Which foods contain the most fat? Which can you eat at no cost to your health? And which should you avoid at *all* costs?

This handbook will enable you to realistically monitor your level of dietary fat consumption. Based on what Americans eat regularly—not just on "good" foods—it offers a wide range of sensible food choices to help you make minor or major changes in your diet as you see fit.

Did you know that . . .

• selecting tortilla chips instead of potato or corn chips will save you 20 calories and 4 grams of fat per ounce, and selecting "light" tortilla chips will save you 40 calories and 6 grams of fat?

• dry-roasted nuts have about the same amount of fat as oil-roasted ones, and that sunflower seeds, widely regarded as a healthful low-fat food, are every bit as fatty as peanuts?

• meats with the word "chopped" in their name, such as "chopped ham," are almost always the fattiest form of that meat you can buy?

With so much useful information at your fingertips, it will only be a matter of minutes before you're . . .

EATING LEANER AND LIGHTER

EATING LEANER
⤜ *and* ⤛
LIGHTER

Cut Your Dietary Fat by 25% or More—Easily, Quickly, Today!

DAVID G. SCHARDT

WARNER BOOKS

A Time Warner Company

This book is not intended as a substitute for medical advice. You are advised to consult regularly with your health care professional in matters relating to your health, and particularly regarding matters which may require diagnosis or medical attention.

All information contained in this book regarding brand name products is based on research by the author which is accurate as of December, 1993.

If you purchase this book without a cover you should be aware that this book may have been stolen property and reported as "unsold and destroyed" to the publisher. In such case neither the author nor the publisher has received any payment for this "stripped book."

For Gloria

Contents

INTRODUCTION

BREAKFAST

LUNCH

DINNER

SNACKS AND SWEETS

FLAVORINGS, SAUCES, DRESSINGS, AND CONDIMENTS

BEVERAGES

Introduction

Congratulations! You have in your hands an easy-to-use guide to eating less fat and fewer calories.

Now you can enjoy the better health that good food with less fat can bring without drastically changing the way you now eat. With *Eating Leaner and Lighter,* you can begin immediately to identify familiar foods that contain less fat and fewer calories and easily skim 5, 10, even 25 grams of fat from what you eat.

Consider breakfast. Do you enjoy making pancakes? Did you know that pancakes prepared by adding water to a "complete" mix contain up to 13 grams less fat per serving than ones prepared from mixes to which you add eggs, milk, and oil?

Do you like bacon for breakfast sometimes? Did you know that Canadian bacon contains up to 7 grams less fat per serving than bacon?

How about granola? Did you know that, cup for cup, some muesli cereals contain 21 grams less fat than some granolas?

If you made substitutions like these today—using a "complete" pancake mix and choosing Canadian bacon instead of regular bacon, or replacing your granola with muesli—you could cut 20 grams of fat from your diet in one meal. That's more than most people need to do throughout the entire day in order to meet the current health recommendations about how much fat to consume. And that's just breakfast!

It's that easy—but only if you know which foods to select. Now, with *Eating Leaner and Lighter,* you have the help you need.

The following sections provide some background information on fat and on how to use this book. But if you can't wait to cut fat, just start browsing through the book. Your choices are organized according to meals and types of foods. *Bon appétit!*

Why Eat Less Fat?

Health authorities are nearly unanimous in their opinion that the most dangerous substance in our food today is not a food additive, nor a pesticide, nor a preservative, nor even food contamination.

No, the number one concern is the fat in our food.

Why? Thousands of scientific studies from all over the world have shown that eating too much fat does the following:

- Increases the risk of developing many types of cancers, especially deadly ones like breast and colon cancer;
- Increases the likelihood that some cancers, such as prostate cancer, may spread throughout the body;
- Increases the likelihood of developing coronary heart disease, the number one cause of death in the United States; and
- Increases the likelihood of becoming overweight, because our bodies store fat in food as excess weight more readily than they store any other source of food energy.

How Much Fat Do We Eat Now?

The average adult woman between ages twenty and sixty in the United States eats about 65 to 70 grams of fat a day, the average adult man about 110 to 115 grams. (Older men and women eat slightly less.)

The amount of fat we eat is often measured as the percent of all the calories in our food it provides. For American adults, fat accounts for about 35 percent to 38 percent of calories consumed. Protein provides 15 percent to 17 percent, carbohydrates 45 percent to 48 percent, and alcohol about 5 percent.

How Much Fat Should We Eat?

Most health authorities recommend that Americans get no more than 30 percent of their calories from fat. That doesn't mean this goal must be reached at each meal or even every day. But over a long period of time, we shouldn't average more than that.

Thirty percent of calories means the average American man should be eating no more than 65 to 100 grams of fat, with older men needing the lower amounts. That's about 20 to 25 grams less than American men currently eat.

For the average American woman, 30 percent of calories translates into 50 to 65 grams of fat a day, with older women needing the lower amounts. That's about 15 grams less than American women currently eat.

Eating 15 to 25 fewer grams of fat a day is easy to do if you have *Eating Leaner and Lighter* to help you.

Here are two simple ways to calculate the number of grams of fat that should be your own daily limit:

First, take the ideal body weight for your size and divide it in half. The result is roughly the maximum number of grams of fat a day you should be eating if you want 30 percent or less of your calories to be from fat. For example, if your healthy body weight should be about 125 pounds, then half of that number, 63, is the maximum number of grams of fat you should be eating. If your healthy body weight should be about 180 pounds, then 90 grams of fat should be your goal.

The second way to calculate the amount of fat you should be eating uses the number of calories you eat in a day. Admittedly, not many people know this number, but if you do, take the total number of calories, drop the right-most digit, and divide by 3. That gives you the number of grams of fat that equals 30 percent of your daily calories. For example, suppose you eat 2,100 calories in a day. Drop the right-most number, 0, which leaves 210. Divide 210 by 3, which gives you 70—70 grams of fat.

Where's the Fat?

Where is the fat in our food? Some of it is obvious, such as margarine and oils. Some of it is not so obvious, like the fat in ramen soups, chili, and muffins.

The leading sources of fat in the American diet are fats and oils eaten as butter, margarine, vegetable oil, and salad dressings, and when added to other foods, such as pies, cookies, and cakes.

The second leading sources of fat are meat, poultry, and fish. The third are dairy products, including milk and ice cream.

These three categories of food account for 90 percent of the fat in the American diet. Beans, nuts, fruits, vegetables, grains, and eggs account for the remaining 10 percent.

The smartest way to skim the fat from what you eat is to zero in on its principal sources in our food—the fats, oils, and foods that use them as an ingredient, as well as meats, poultry, fish, and dairy products.

How to Use This Book

Eating Leaner and Lighter shows you how to quickly and easily identify foods similar to those you are eating now, but that contain fewer grams of fat and often fewer calories.

The book organizes the thousands of different foods Americans customarily eat into groups of similar products. Within these groups, the foods are arranged in order of their fat content, with the fattiest listed first, then the less fatty, followed by the leaner ones, and finally the leanest.

To use this book, pick a category of food and then look for what you would ordinarily eat or select for your family. Then, look down the page for alternatives with fewer grams of fat that you also like to eat or would consider eating instead. In most cases, you can find choices that are just slightly leaner or ones that are considerably less fatty. The decision is yours to make.

For instance, suppose you would like to eat a soup with noodles. Turn to the page on noodle, rice, barley, and ramen soups in the lunch section. You should avoid most of the ramen soups, which contain up to 18 grams of fat per cup.

However, there are some low-fat ramen soups with just 1 to 2 grams of fat. There's also chunky chicken noodle soup with 5 to 6 grams of fat per cup, or regular chicken noodle with 1 to 4 grams. Or how about wonton soup, with only 1 gram?

See how easy it is? Do that for more foods and watch your fat savings add up. It won't be long before you reach the 15 to 25 grams of fat most Americans should be skimming from what they eat.

Different Ways to Use
This Book

Eating Leaner and Lighter is so simple to use that anyone can begin immediately to use it to pare some of the fat from their meals. You don't need medical supervision or a special diet. You don't have to commit yourself to a grand overhaul of your menus. You don't have to resign yourself to eating unfamiliar or unsatisfying foods.

You can shave off a little here and there, now and again. Or, you can systematically reduce the fat in your foods, every meal, every day. The choice is yours. But either way, you'll be taking the right steps to a healthier diet.

And you'll be doing it in a sensible way. Experts know that a steady, step-by-step change is often more successful and permanent than a sudden lurch into a new direction, especially in matters as personal as what we like to eat.

If you are responsible for preparing the meals for your family, you can use *Eating Leaner and Lighter* to slowly and quietly introduce less fatty foods without inciting a revolt. That's because *Eating Leaner and Lighter* identifies a range of similar and familiar foods to choose from. You can pick those that are slightly leaner, or ones that are vastly leaner, depending upon how picky your family is.

If you are following a diet plan, one prescribed by a physician, nutritionist, dietitian, or other qualified health professional, you can use *Eating Leaner and Lighter* to keep your meals interesting and varied. The amounts of saturated fat and sodium in foods are provided here to help you. Of course, check with your professional before making changes in a diet assigned you.

You can also use *Eating Leaner and Lighter* to evaluate the new foods and reformulated products that are being introduced into today's health-conscious marketplace. Judge how a new food product rates by using the groups of foods with their range of fat and calories as a framework.

For instance, suppose you find a new "lite" potato chip with 6 grams of fat in each ounce and you want to know how that stands up to other chips. Just turn to the pages on potato, corn, and tortilla chips and you can quickly see that the new chip is, indeed, less fatty than regular potato chips, but is about the same as regular tortilla chips.

The Nutrient Information on Foods and Where It Comes From

Eating Leaner and Lighter summarizes important nutrient information for thousands of different foods and different brands available in the United States. Included are both national and major regional brands. Of course, not every food product or every brand is represented. But you can use the information here to evaluate the fat content of foods that are not listed.

For each food listed, the calories, total fat in grams (g), percent of calories from fat (%), saturated fat in grams (g) if available, and sodium content in milligrams (mg) are specified. For some foods, the cholesterol level in milligrams (mg) is also listed. The serving sizes are the new realistic ones recently authorized by the Food and Drug Administration.

Saturated fat is a type of fat found in nearly all food, but in the greatest amounts in meat, poultry, and dairy fat. Since it causes blood cholesterol levels to rise, health authorities recommend that American adults consume no more than 20 to 25 grams of saturated fat a day.

Excessive amounts of sodium can raise blood pressure levels, which in turn can lead to heart attacks and strokes. For this reason, health authorities recommend that Americans eat far less sodium than they do now. On the new food labels, the recommended "Daily Value" for sodium is 2,400 milligrams a day.

Cholesterol in food can raise the cholesterol in blood, which increases the risk of coronary heart disease. Although medical authorities recommend that Americans consume no more than 300 milligrams of cholesterol a day, most experts believe that *saturated fat is more significant* in raising blood cholesterol levels.

The nutrient information in *Eating Leaner and Lighter* was obtained from food companies, official government data, and scientific research. Every attempt has been made to keep this information accurate and up-to-date. However, companies do reformulate their products from time to time, so if the exact nutrient content is very important to your health, you should rely on the companies' current nutrition labels.

The New Nutrition Labels: Where to Locate the Information About Fat

Most foods in supermarkets will carry new nutrition labels on their packages beginning in May, 1994. Each label will specify the amount of fat, saturated fat, and cholesterol, as well as the total number of calories derived from fat in a serving of the food. In addition, the label will indicate how much of a day's recommended maximum amount of fat, saturated fat, and cholesterol the food provides. Here's where to locate this information:

1. The amount of fat per serving of the food (the serving size is described near the top of the label).

2. The amount of saturated fat per serving of the food.

3. The amount of cholesterol per serving of the food.

4. The number of calories derived from fat in the food. To learn the percent of calories from fat, which is not mandatory on the new labels, divide this number by the total number of calories in a serving and multiply by 100. In this illustration,

120 divided by 260, times 100, equals 46 percent of the food's calories from fat.

5. The percent of a day's maximum amount of fat recommended for good health, based on a 2,000 calorie diet. This is *not* the percent of calories from fat in the food. "Daily Value" is the new standard on labels for healthy diets, replacing the USRDAs. Labels may contain standards for both 2,000- and 2,500-calorie diets. Your particular needs may be more or less than this.

6. The percent of a day's maximum amount of saturated fat recommended for good health, based on a 2,000-calorie diet.

7. The percent of a day's maximum amount of cholesterol, based on a 2,000-calorie diet.

In addition to this information, new standards for what can be called "fat-free," "low-fat," "reduced-fat," and "light" or "lite" are also being introduced.

In general, a product can be labeled "fat-free" only if it contains less than half a gram of fat per serving. Most foods labeled "low-fat" must contain 3 grams of fat or less per serving. "Reduced-fat" or "lower fat" foods have had their fat content lowered by at least 25 percent. "Light" or "lite" foods must contain either at least a third fewer calories or no more than half the fat of the regular product.

Nutrition Facts

Serving Size 1 cup (228g)
Servings Per Container 2

Amount Per Serving

Calories 260　　　　　Calories from Fat 120

　　　　　　　　　　　　　　　% Daily Value*

Total Fat 13g	**20%**
Saturated Fat 5g	**25%**
Cholesterol 30mg	**10%**
Sodium 660mg	**28%**
Total Carbohydrate 31g	**10%**
Dietary Fiber 0g	**0%**
Sugars 5g	
Protein 5g	

Vitamin A 4%	•	Vitamin C 2%
Calcium 15%	•	Iron 4%

*Percent Daily Values are based on a 2,000-calorie diet. Your daily values may be higher or lower depending on your calorie needs:

	Calories:	2,000	2,500
Total Fat	Less than	65g	80g
Sat Fat	Less than	20g	25g
Cholesterol	Less than	300mg	300mg
Sodium	Less than	2,400mg	2,400mg
Total Carbohydrate		300g	375g
Dietary Fiber		25g	30g

Calories per gram:
Fat 9　•　Carbohydrates 4　•　Protein 4

EATING
LEANER
❖ and ❖
LIGHTER

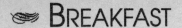 BREAKFAST

grains
ready-to-eat breakfast cereals
hot breakfast cereals
bread
biscuits
muffins and quick breads
pancakes
waffles and french toast

eggs, meats, and potatoes
eggs and egg substitutes
breakfast meats: bacon, sausage, ham and other meats
hot side dishes: hash, hash browns, and grits
breakfast sandwiches

sweets
breakfast pastry to be heated
instant breakfasts: bars and milk mixes

grains

Ready-to-eat Breakfast Cereals

Grains, and most breakfast cereals made from them, are naturally low in fat. However, there are some exceptions, where manufacturers add enough vegetable oils and other ingredients to make them as fatty as many meats. These exceptions are listed among the "fattiest" and "less fatty" choices that follow. Meanwhile, note what does and does not affect the fat content of cereals.

things that affect the fat content:
addition of vegetable oil: most granolas and some high-fiber cereals have extra vegetable fat added to make them more palatable

   addition of nuts: extra nuts in cereal will increase the fat content—every three almonds, or the equivalent amount of other nuts, adds 2 grams of fat

   use of oats: since oats contain more fat than the other grains commonly used to make breakfast cereal, oat cereals will tend to have more fat

things that do not affect the fat content:
addition of dried fruit: fruit is fat-free, but it will drive the calories up

frosted versus unfrosted cereals: frosted versions contain the same amount of fat and calories, ounce for ounce, as the unfrosted versions of the cereals

NOTE: All the information on breakfast cereals listed is based on a *one-cup* serving, even though many cereals specify different serving sizes on their packages. The reason is that most people pour cereal by visual volume, not by any official serving size on the carton. By listing all the cereals with one serving size, the differences in their calories and fat became more obvious.

Remember: the % of fat formula is grams of fat multiplied by nine and divided by total calories.

the fattiest . . .

food (one-cup serving)	cals	fat (g)	fat (%)	sat (g)	sodium (mg)
most granolas	380-530	15-24	28-42	2-16	10-560

Regular granolas have by far the most fat of any breakfast cereal. Several companies now offer lower-fat or even fat-free granolas, as you will see.

the less fatty . . .

food (one-cup serving)	cals	fat (g)	fat (%)	sat (g)	sodium (mg)
Kellogg's crunchy oat brans	220-335	6-9	25	2-3	280-575
most mueslis	240-440	3-8	11-19	0	0-340
some lower-fat granolas	260-360	2-6	7-15	0	180-375

The **Kellogg's crunchy oat bran cereals** include Oatbake and Cracklin' Oat Bran. **Mueslis** contain less added fat than granolas. The **lower-fat granola** brands include Familia, Kellogg, Post Bran'nola, and Quaker Oats.

the leaner . . .

food (one-cup serving)	cals	fat (g)	fat (%)	sat (g)	sodium (mg)
some oat cereals	110-210	2-4	13-30	0-2	0-470
many Quaker Oats cereals	150-160	2-4	14-23	0-1	225-375
many bran cereals	100-235	0-3	0-16	0-1	0-865

These **oat cereals** include Kellogg's Oat Squares, New Morning Oatios, and such **Quaker Oats cereals** as Ohs!, Cap'n Crunch, and Life.

the leanest . . .

food (one-cup serving)	cals	fat (g)	fat (%)	sat (g)	sodium (mg)
most ready-to-eat cereals	50-200	0-1	0-15	1	5-435
fat-free granolas	360	0	0	0	80

Most **ready-to-eat cereals** contain little, if any, fat. These include products such as shredded wheat, Chex, Rice Krispies, corn flakes, wheat flakes, Cheerios, puffed cereals, and flakes made from other grains. Health Valley is a national brand of **fat-free granola.**

fat-skimming tips:
   • use the leanest milk you can on your cereal, because this usually determines the total amount of fat in your cereal bowl more than anything else

   • choose muesli over granola

see these pages for:
   238 milks to pour on cereal
   161 dried fruits to add
   197 fresh fruits to add
   217 sweeteners to use
     6 hot breakfast cereals

cals=calories; fat=grams of fat; %fat=percent of calories from fat; sat=grams of saturated fat; sodium=milligrams of sodium

Hot Breakfast Cereals
Nearly all of the hot breakfast cereals, like the ready-to-eat ones, are low in fat because they are made from grains. Hot cereals often have the additional advantage of being less processed than ready-to-eat cold cereals.

things that affect the fat content:
flavoring with nuts or coconut: these fatty ingredients raise the cereal's fat content

substitution of plain hot bran or germ: these contain more

fat than cereals made from the starchy part of grain because plants store their fat in the bran and germ

use of oats: since oats contain more fat than the other grains commonly used for breakfast cereal, oatmeal will have slightly more fat than wheat, corn, or rice cereals

flavoring with cheese, butter, or ham: these flavors raise the fat level of grits

things that do not affect the fat content:
sweet or spicy flavorings: honey, maple, cinnamon, and other such flavors may add calories but do not affect the fat content

regular versus quick–cooking versus instant: how fast the cereal can absorb cooking water does not affect the fat content

the fattiest . . .

food (one-cup serving)	cals	fat (g)	fat (%)	sat (g)	sodium (mg)
oatmeals flavored with nuts or coconut	220-250	5-8	19-32	0-5	5-515

Brands of **flavored oatmeals** include Roman Meal and Arrowhead Mills.

the less fatty . . .

food (one-cup serving)	cals	fat (g)	fat (%)	sat (g)	sodium (mg)
plain wheat germ, wheat bran, or oat bran	130-150	3-4	18-26	0-1	0-5

The **germ** and **bran** is where the grain stores its fat.

the leaner . . .

food (one-cup serving)	cals	fat (g)	fat (%)	sat (g)	sodium (mg)
grits flavored with ham/butter/cheese	180-200	2-4	9-18	0	700-1240
oatmeal with sweet or spicy flavors	135-245	2-3	11-14	0-1	140-425
plain	110-155	2-3	12-18	0-1	0-375

Oatmeal contains slightly more fat than other grains. Note the high sodium levels in flavored grits.

the leanest . . .

food (one-cup serving)	cals	fat (g)	fat (%)	sat (g)	sodium (mg)
most hot wheat, rice, and rye cereals flavored	135-205	0-1	0-12	0	280-390
plain	105-155	0-1	0-10	0	0-405
plain grits	135-140	0-1	0-5	0	0-605

These **hot cereals** include the creams of rice, wheat, and rye; and whole wheat, farina, and multigrain cereals. The flavored varieties may contain more calories, but not more fat, than the plain kinds.

fat-skimming tips:
- Use the leanest milk you can on your cereal, because this usually determines the total amount of fat in your cereal bowl more than anything else.

• Skip cereals with nuts, coconut, ham, butter, or cheese.

see these pages for:
   238 milks to pour on cereal
   161 dried fruits to add
   197 fresh fruits to add
   217 sweeteners to use
     3 ready-to-eat breakfast cereals

cal=calories; fat=grams of fat; %fat=percent of calories from fat; sat=grams of saturated fat; sodium=milligrams of sodium

Bread

Most breads are low in fat because they are prepared from low-fat ingredients, such as flour, water, sugar, and yeast. The most significant source of fat is likely to be what you spread on the bread or put between sandwich slices.

this affects the fat content:
use of whole grain: sometimes whole wheat, cracked wheat, oat bran, and other types of bread that contain the whole grain have slightly more fat than refined breads, but whole grain breads are also richer in vitamins and minerals

things that do not affect the fat content:
source of grain: wheat, rye, and other flours all have very little fat (oats have more fat than other grains, but not enough in two slices of bread to matter that much)

sourdough fermentation: fermentation by sourdough bacteria has no effect on the fat content of bread or English muffins

presence of caraway seeds, dill, onion bits, and cracked wheat kernels: dill and onions have no fat, and there are not

enough seeds or wheat kernels in two slices of bread to affect
the fat content

addition of egg: some breads, such as challah, contain more
fat because of the addition of egg yolks

the fattiest . . .

food (two slices or two ounces)	cals	fat (g)	fat (%)	sat (g)	sodium (mg)
Pepperidge Farm cinnamon swirl bread	180	6	30	0	220
Arnold's Bran'nola oat bread	180	6	30	0	260
egg bread	160	5	19	1	280

**Pepperidge Farm cinnamon swirl bread and Arnold's
Bran'nola oat bread** are two of the fattiest sliced breads
available nationally. This extra fat comes from vegetable shortening added to the dough.

other choices with the most calories . . .

food (one bagel)	cals	fat (g)	fat (%)	sat (g)	sodium (mg)
bagels large-size (4-inch diameter)	245	1	4-9	0	475
medium-size (3.5-inch diameter)	195	1	4-9	0	380

These **bagels** have more calories—but not more fat—than
most other breads only because they are bigger than two slices
of bread.

the choices with fewer calories . . .

food (one bagel or two slices)	cals	fat (g)	fat (%)	sat (g)	sodium (mg)
most breads	130-140	2	13-14	0-1	130-300
bagel, small-size (3-inch diameter)	155	1	4-9	0	305
English muffin	135-150	1	4-8	0	200-420

These **breads** are the wheat, whole wheat, white, cracked wheat, French, Vienna, Italian, mixed grains, oatmeal, pumpernickel, raisin, rye, and similar varieties. A **3-inch diameter bagel** is the equivalent of two slices of bread.

the choices with the least calories . . .

food (two slices)	cals	fat (g)	fat (%)	sat (g)	sodium (mg)
lower-calorie breads	80-100	0-1	0-11	0	80-115

These new **lower-calorie breads** are formulated with extra fiber (which has no calories) to replace some of the starch (which does have calories). Some brands are Wonder, Schmidt, Arnold, Oatmeal Goodness, Weight Watchers, Hollywood, Blue Ribbon, Roman Meal, Pepperidge Farm, and many others.

fat-skimming tip:
- what you spread on your bread or put between sandwich slices will probably contain more fat than the bread itself

see these pages for:
203 butter, margarine, or vegetable oil spreads

218 jelly, preserves, jam, or honey
  47 peanut butter, tuna fish, and other sandwich spreads
  53 sandwich meats
226 mustard and other hot or spicy spreads

cals=calories; fat=grams of fat; %fat=percent of calories from fat; sat=grams of
saturated fat; sodium=milligrams of sodium

Biscuits
Hot biscuits for breakfast conjure up images of hearty morning meals served by loving cooks. However, as with many other foods, the fat content can vary significantly.

this affects the fat content:
size: biscuits come in a variety of sizes, and that determines their fat content more than anything else

things that do not affect the fat content:
flavoring with butter or buttermilk: first, it's usually not real butter or traditional buttermilk and, second, too little is used to matter much anyway

  southern-style, Texas-style, baking powder, or flaky-style: these have no more fat or calories than other kinds of biscuits.

the fattiest . . .

food (one)	cals	fat (g)	fat (%)	sat (g)	sodium (mg)
fast-food biscuit	230-320	12-17	45-49	3-6	510-730

Biscuits in the clutches of the **fast-food restaurants** suffer the same fate as many other foods: they become fattier than they should be. These are the rough equivalent in calories and fat of two slices of bread and a tablespoon of butter or margarine.

the less fatty . . .

food (one)	cals	fat (g)	fat (%)	sat (g)	sodium (mg)
homemade plain or buttermilk biscuit	210	10	42	3	350
large biscuit prepared from mix or refrigerated dough	140-200	8-10	33-48	2-3	305-580
medium biscuit prepared from mix or refrigerated dough	90-130	2-5	24-50	0-1	195-320

A **large biscuit** weighs about two ounces. Pillsbury Grands! and Pillsbury "Big Premium" are examples.

A **medium biscuit** weighs about an ounce. Pillsbury's Hungry Jack and 1869 are examples.

the leanest . . .

food (one)	cals	fat (g)	fat (%)	sat (g)	sodium (mg)
from refrigerated dough small biscuit	50	1	9-18	0-1	165-410

Small biscuits, which weigh about two-thirds of an ounce, are often a supermarket's own brand.

fat-skimming tips:
- bread is far leaner than biscuits

- some biscuits are visibly greasy and can be blotted with a napkin

- a careful choice of what to spread on, pour over, or eat with your biscuit can keep it from becoming the equivalent of a hamburger

see these pages for:
203 butter, margarine, or vegetable oil spreads
218 jelly, jam, or preserves
228 gravy
 34 fast-food sandwiches with biscuits
 14 muffins

cals=calories; fat=grams of fat; %fat=percent of calories from fat; sat=grams of saturated fat; sodium=milligrams of sodium

Muffins and Quick Breads
Muffins and quick breads have the image of being wholesome, delicious, small packages of nutritious ingredients. Some are just that, but others more closely resemble cake.

things that affect the fat content:
size: some muffins are now nearly the size of a lumberjack's fist—bigger means fattier

flavoring with nuts or chocolate: these high-fat ingredients raise the muffin's fat as well

addition of bran: bran muffins are sometimes, but not always, lower in fat than other varieties

things that do not affect the fat content:
flavoring with fruit: banana, blueberry, or other fruit flavors do
not affect the fat or calorie content

source of the grain: most muffins are made primarily from
wheat or corn flour, which are similar in their calorie and fat
contents

the fattiest . . .

food (one)	cals	fat (g)	fat (%)	sat (g)	sodium (mg)
fast-food muffins					
Hardee's	400	17	38	4	310
Burger King	290	14	43	3	245
Dunkin' Donuts	280-340	8-12	26-32	1-2	340-560
Carl's Jr.	310-340	7-9	20-24	0-1	300-370
Arby's	240	7	26	1	200
higher-fat brand-name muffins	240-420	10-16	21-55	2	160-540

Muffins sold by fast-food restaurants are among the fattiest you can buy, in part because these tend to be quite large.
The one major exception is the fat-free muffins sold in
McDonald's restaurants, which are listed in "the leanest" category. Examples of **higher-fat brand-name muffins**
include Hostess "Mini" muffins and some Sara Lee's frozen
muffins.

the less fatty . . .

food (one)	cals	fat (g)	fat (%)	sat (g)	sodium (mg)
frozen medium-fat muffins	170-220	6-8	32-37	2	200-280
most medium-fat ready-to-eat muffins	100-360	4-8	16-39	0-1	135-650
muffins prepared from regular mixes	110-210	3-9	23-45	1-2	140-395

Frozen medium-fat muffins include some Sara Lee and Pepperidge Farm products. Medium-fat ready-to-eat muffins include Arnold and Entenmann's brands. Duncan Hines, Jiffy, Betty Crocker, and Martha White are examples of muffins prepared from regular mixes, to which are added milk, eggs, and oil, and are not marketed as lite.

the leaner . . .

food (one slice)	cals	fat (g)	fat (%)	sat (g)	sodium (mg)
quick breads prepared from mixes	115-190	3-7	17-33	0-2	150-490

Quick breads—Pillsbury, Gold Medal, Ballard, and Arrowhead Mills brands, among others—are available in flavors ranging from corn, banana, and oatmeal raisin to nut, cranberry, date, and apple-cinnamon.

the leanest . . .

food (one)	cals	fat (g)	fat (%)	sat (g)	sodium (mg)
muffins prepared "lite" from mixes	100-200	2-8	16-36	1-2	140-300
lower-fat frozen muffins	120-190	0-6	0-30	0-1	90-250
low-fat or fat-free muffins	100-150	0-1	0-9	0-1	80-290
McDonald's fat-free muffins	170-180	0	0	0	200-220

Muffins can be prepared "lite" from Betty Crocker, Duncan Hines, General Mills, and Washington mixes, among others, by using skim milk and egg whites (the directions are usually on the box). **Lower-fat frozen muffins** are available from Weight Watchers, Healthy Choice, Pepperidge Farm Wholesome Choice, and the Free & Light line of Sara Lee.

Low-fat muffins with 1 gram or less of fat are available from Pillsbury's Lovin' Lites mix and Hostess, which has a line of 97% fat-free muffins. Health Valley and Entenmann's sell **fat-free muffins,** as does McDonald's.

cals=calories; fat=grams of fat; %fat=percent of calories from fat; sat=grams of saturated fat; sodium=milligrams of sodium

Pancakes

Whether you call them pancakes, hotcakes, flapjacks, griddle cakes, or any of the other colorful names Americans have given to these quick breads, they are one of this country's favorite breakfast foods.

Although pancakes consist of a fairly standard mixture of flour, water, eggs, milk, and baking powder, there are surprising differences in the fat content of the pancakes you can buy.

things that affect the fat content:
complete versus regular mixes: pancakes prepared from complete mixes to which you add only water usually contain less fat than pancakes made from regular mixes to which you add milk and eggs. That's because the complete mixes use non-fat milk and egg whites as ingredients.

flavoring with nuts: nuts in the pancakes increase the fat content

things that do not affect the fat content:

use of buckwheat or buttermilk: buckwheat is similar to wheat, and buttermilk contains little fat, so these flavors do not affect the fat or calorie content of pancakes

flavoring with blueberry or other fruits: since fruits are fat-free, these also do not affect the fat or calorie content

use of whole grains: pancakes made from whole wheat flour contain about the same amount of fat and calories as pancakes made from refined flour

the fattiest . . .

food (three 4-inch pancakes)	cals	fat (g)	fat (%)	sat (g)	sodium (mg)
fast-food pancakes	205-275	6-14	26-46	1-2	570-920
pancakes prepared from regular mixes	190-320	6-14	26-39	1-3	480-860

Pancakes from fast-food restaurants are among the fattiest available. But they've got company. Pancakes prepared from **regular dry mixes,** such as Hungry Jack, Bisquick (even the new fat-reduced kind), and Aunt Jemima—to which you add the milk, eggs, and sometimes oil—contain as much fat as the fast-food ones. The lesson is to buy the *complete* mixes, the ones to which you add just water.

the less fatty . . .

food (three 4-inch pancakes)	cals	fat (g)	fat (%)	sat (g)	sodium (mg)
frozen pancakes	210-260	4-5	13-19	0-1	545-840
pancakes prepared "lite" from regular mixes	170-200	3-7	16-32	0-1	500-600

Brands of **frozen pancakes,** ready for heating in a microwave oven, include Aunt Jemima and Pillsbury's Hungry Jack. **Preparing pancakes "lite" from regular mixes** can reduce the fat content by half compared to pancakes made with whole eggs, whole milk, and vegetable oil. Follow the "lite" directions on the boxes of brands such as Hungry Jack and Aunt Jemima to substitute egg whites, low-fat or skim milk, and little or no oil.

the leanest . . .

food (three 4-inch pancakes)	cals	fat (g)	fat (%)	sat (g)	sodium (mg)
pancakes made from "lite" mixes	130-230	0-3	0-13	0	90-570
pancakes made from "complete" mixes	180-250	1-3	5-15	0-1	500-880
frozen low-fat pancakes	140	2	13	0	620

"Lite" pancake mixes, such as Aunt Jemima, Arrowhead Mills, Featherweight, and Estee brands, are specially formulated to contain less fat and calories. **Pancakes prepared from complete mixes,** to which you add only water or merely thaw and pour, contain substantially less fat than other pancakes because they use non-fat milk and egg whites as ingredients. Some of these brands are Aunt Jemima frozen batter, Bisquick's Shake 'N Pour, Hungry Jack, Betty Crocker, and Featherweight. Aunt Jemima is also a brand of **frozen low-fat pancakes.**

fat-skimming tips:
- look for complete pancake mixes

- use skim milk, egg whites, and little or no oil when preparing pancake batter

see these pages for:
  219 syrups and fruit toppings
  203 butter, margarine, and vegetable oil spreads
  20 waffles and French toast

cals=calories; fat=grams of fat; %fat=percent of calories from fat; sat=grams of saturated fat; sodium=milligrams of sodium

Waffles and French Toast
Here are two popular alternatives to pancakes. However, a serving of French toast will usually contain more fat than a serving of waffles, and either one will usually provide more fat than a serving of pancakes.

things that affect the fat content:
deep-frying: French toast that has been deep-fried, the way fast-food restaurants cook it, will have much more fat than French toast fried in a pan

frozen varieties versus mixes: waffles and French toast that are ready to heat in the microwave usually will have less fat than waffles prepared at home from mixes or than French toast made from scratch

complete versus regular mixes: waffles prepared from complete mixes to which you add only water will usually contain less fat than those prepared from mixes to which you add your own eggs, milk, and oil

size of the waffles: waffles come in a variety of sizes, with the larger ones containing, naturally, more fat. Large waffles measure about 4 inches in diameter and weigh about 40 grams. Medium waffles measure about 4 inches square and weigh about 35 grams. And small waffles measure about 4 inches by 3 inches and weigh 25 to 30 grams.

this does not affect the fat content:
Belgian versus regular waffles. Belgian waffles may be bigger and thicker than regular waffles, but ounce for ounce these have the same amount of fat.

the fattiest . . .

food (one serving)	cals	fat (g)	fat (%)	sat (g)	sodium (mg)
fast-food French toast	480-540	26-32	48-55	5-6	500-620

Predictably, French toast prepared in fast-food restaurants tends to be the fattiest available. It's essentially fried bread and contains about twice the amount of fat as a serving of pancakes.

the less fatty . . .

food (one serving)	cals	fat (g)	fat (%)	sat (g)	sodium (mg)
homemade French toast with 2% milk	300	14	42	4	620
waffles					
from regular mix (2 small)	190-260	8-14	37-52	2	350-630
frozen (2 large)	220-260	8-12	30-42	1-2	400-500
frozen w/fruit topping (1 large)	380	12	28	2	460-500
from complete mix (2 small)	190-280	6-12	19-52	1-2	400-700

Regular waffle mixes and complete waffle mixes include brands from Aunt Jemima, Hungry Jack, Bisquick, and Mrs. Butterworth's. Frozen large waffles are available from Eggo or Nutri-Grain. Note that two large frozen waffles are comparable in calories and fat to two small ones prepared from a mix.

the leaner . . .

food (one serving or 3 oz)	cals	fat (g)	fat (%)	sat (g)	sodium (mg)
frozen French toast	130-380	4-8	19-55	1-2	280-585
waffles					
frozen (2 medium)	170-180	2-6	13-30	0	160-570
frozen (2 small)	120-150	4	23	0	135-210
frozen (2 mini)	50-90	2-4	30-34	0	100-210

Frozen French toast is available from Aunt Jemima and Downyflake. Examples of frozen waffle brands include

Downyflake, Van's, and Special K, as well as many store brands.

the leanest . . .

food (one serving)	cals	fat (g)	fat (%)	sat (g)	sodium (mg)
frozen low-fat waffles (2 medium)	120-140	2	13-15	0	460-480
frozen fat-free waffles (2 small)	160	0	0	0	260

Frozen low-fat waffles are available from Aunt Jemima and Belgian Chef. Kellogg's Special K is a brand of frozen fat-free waffles.

fat-skimming tips:

• skip the French toast

• if you do make French toast at home, use an egg substitute instead of whole eggs

• look for frozen waffles and French toast rather than mixes

see these pages for:

203 butter or margarine
219 syrups and toppings
17 pancakes
24 egg substitutes

cals=calories; fat=grams of fat; %fat=percent of calories from fat; sat=grams of saturated fat; sodium=milligrams of sodium

eggs, meats, and potatoes

Eggs and Egg Substitutes

Egg consumption continues to drop in the United States, as it has ever since World War II. Health experts think this is because Americans are concerned about cholesterol, whereas the egg industry insists the reason is that Americans seldom take the time to make hot breakfasts with eggs.

this affects the fat content:
size of egg: the bigger the egg, the bigger the yolk—and that's where all the fat and cholesterol are

things that do not affect the fat content:

color of the shell: the only difference between brown and white eggs is the color of the shells

free-range or organic farming: all eggs, regardless of the chickens' environment, have the same fat, cholesterol, and calories

fertilization: fertilized eggs also have the same fat, cholesterol, and calories

the fattiest . . .

food (one egg)	cals	fat (g)	fat (%)	sat (g)	chol (mg)	sodium (mg)
jumbo	100	7	61	2	280	80
extra large	90	6	61	2	255	70

the less fatty . . .

food (one egg)	cals	fat (g)	fat (%)	sat (g)	chol (mg)	sodium (mg)
large	75	5	61	2	215	65
large "reduced cholesterol"	70	5	64	2	45	125
medium	70	5	61	1	190	55
small	60	4	61	1	165	45

"Reduced cholesterol" eggs are liquid eggs, packaged in cartons, from which most of the cholesterol—but not the fat—have been spun away. Simply Eggs is one national brand.

the leaner . . .

food (equivalent to one large egg)	cals	fat (g)	fat (%)	sat (g)	chol (mg)	sodium (mg)
higher-fat egg substitutes	60	2-4	30-60	0-1	0	90-125
lower-fat egg substitutes	15-40	0-1	0-15	0	0	90-115

Egg substitutes consist primarily of egg whites to which are added a little bit of vegetable oil, yellow coloring, additives, and nutrients. They can be used for making scrambled eggs, omelets, and most other dishes requiring eggs, including baked foods. Because the yolk is discarded, these products contain none of the egg's fat or cholesterol. **Higher-fat egg substitutes** use larger amounts of vegetable oil to replace the yolk, and thus contain more fat. Brands include Second Nature, Egg Scramblers, and Featherweight dry eggs. The **lower-fat egg substitutes** use lesser amounts of vegetable oil. These include Healthy Choice, Egg Beaters, Better 'n Eggs, Lyle Farms, Sunny Fresh, and other brands.

the leanest . . .

food (from one large egg)	cals	fat (g)	fat (%)	sat (g)	chol (mg)	sodium (mg)
one egg white	15	0	0	0	0	50

Plain egg whites contain the least amount of calories, fat, and cholesterol. You can make your own egg substitute by removing the yolks from several eggs and then adding back to the whites a little of the yolk for flavor and color.

fat-skimming tips:
  • poach or hard-cook for a leaner way of cooking eggs

  • be careful of eggs from most birds other than chickens, because these have more calories, fat, and cholesterol than chicken eggs. A goose egg has 265 calories, 19 grams of fat, and about 1,275 mg of cholesterol; a duck egg 130 calories, 10 grams of fat, and 620 mg of cholesterol; and a turkey egg 135 calories, 9 grams of fat, and 735 mg of cholesterol.

cals=calories; fat=grams of fat; %fat=percent of calories from fat; sat=grams of saturated fat; sodium=milligrams of sodium

Breakfast Meats: Bacon, Sausage, Ham, and Other Meats

Salty, fatty meats have been a popular food on breakfast tables for centuries. However, the era is long gone for most of us when such meats are necessary to keep us feeling satisfied until the mid-day meal. Fortunately, today there are some lower-fat alternatives available.

things that affect the fat content:

use of turkey meat: sausage or bacon made with turkey meat instead of pork or beef will contain *less* fat

mixing in grain: breakfast meats with grain mixed in, such as scrapple and some "lite" sausage, have less fat because the grain is leaner than the meat and fat that it displaces

cut of pork: bacon cut from the belly of a pig will contain more fat than either Canadian bacon, cut from the loin, or ham, cut from the buttock and thigh

things that do not affect the fat content:

shape of the sausage: links and patties have the same amount of fat and calories

pre-cooking: brown-and-serve sausage that has been pre-cooked and needs only re-heating has the same fat and calories as sausage that is freshly cooked

packaging for the microwave oven: bacon packaged for microwaving, such as Hormel brand, has the same fat and calories as bacon intended for frying

the fattiest . . .

food (about 2 oz.)	cals	fat (g)	fat (%)	sat (g)	chol (mg)	sodium (mg)
pork sausage in links or patties	190-255	17-26	76-90	6-10	20-60	320-635

Pork sausage is one of the fattiest meats you can eat. Federal regulations allow manufacturers to let fat make up half the weight in raw breakfast sausage. Even the much-criticized hot dog has a maximum of 30 percent fat by weight.

the less fatty . . .

food (2 oz. sausage/half-ounce bacon)	cals	fat (g)	fat (%)	sat (g)	chol (mg)	sodium (mg)
"lite" pork sausage	105-145	7-12	40-75	5-6	40-60	310-705
scrapple	115	8	31	3	30	295
"meatless" sausage	110-140	6-9	50-57	1	0	365-515
bacon	70-95	6-8	60-77	2-3	10-15	240-760
turkey breakfast sausage	85-120	4-8	40-62	1-2	30-50	355-705

"Lite" pork sausage is made with pork and turkey meat, or with pork and rice. Brands include Jimmy Dean and Jones Dairy Farm. **Scrapple,** a traditional food of the German and Dutch settlers of Pennsylvania, consists of meat byproducts mixed with cornmeal or another grain. **"Meatless" sausage** is manufactured from soybean protein to resemble meat. Morningstar Farms is a national brand.

A serving of **bacon** has considerably less fat than a serving of pork sausage—if the amount eaten is limited to what the USDA has specified is one typical serving of bacon, about 15 grams or one-half ounce. That's equivalent to two or three medium-size slices of cooked bacon.

Turkey breakfast sausage is substantially leaner than pork sausage for two main reasons. First, turkey meat is naturally leaner than pork. Second, manufacturers of processed meats usually mix in less fat with turkey or chicken than they do with beef or pork. That's because the taste of processed poultry meat becomes unacceptable if too much fat is added. Brands of turkey sausage include Louis Rich, Mr. Turkey, and the Turkey Store.

the leaner . . .

food (about half an ounce)	cals	fat (g)	fat (%)	sat (g)	chol (mg)	sodium (mg)
breakfast "strips"	50-65	4-6	66-77	1-2	15-20	165-355
turkey bacon	40-55	3-4	51-72	1	20-30	335-415

Breakfast "strips" are bacon-like meats fabricated from combinations of pork, beef, and turkey. As you can see, they have one-third less fat than regular bacon. Brands include Sizzlean and Spam. **Turkey bacon** is cured turkey that is fashioned into strips like bacon. It has about half the fat of bacon. National brands include Louis Rich, Mr. Turkey, and Turkey Selects.

the leanest . . .

food (about 2 oz.)	cals	fat (g)	fat (%)	sat (g)	chol (mg)	sodium (mg)
Canadian bacon	60-85	1-4	18-40	0-1	20-30	765-770
lean ham	50-65	1-2	17-31	0-1	40-45	450-870

Lean ham and **Canadian bacon** are the least fatty of the meats commonly eaten for breakfast. Ham in general is leaner than many people think. And Canadian bacon is prepared from the loin of the pig, always one of the least fatty cuts of meat.

fat-skimming tips:
- choose ham or Canadian bacon, when possible

- pat cooked sausage and bacon dry with a paper towel or napkin

see these pages for related foods:
   66 bacon toppings for salads
   53 ham for lunch
   112 ham for dinner

cals=calories; fat=grams of fat; %fat=percent of calories from fat; sat=grams of saturated fat; sodium=milligrams of sodium

Hot Side Dishes: Hash, Hash Browns, and Grits

Hash is an old-fashioned way of making fatty cuts of meats go further by mixing them with a starchy low-fat food like potatoes. Plain potatoes in the form of hash browns and corn in the form of grits are among the most popular side dishes at breakfast.

things that affect the fat content:
type of meat in the hash: corned beef is fattier than roast beef

   use of cheese, butter, and ham flavorings in the grits: flavorings like these added to grits raise its fat level

things that do not affect the fat content:
addition of onions or green peppers to hash: these vegetables do not contain fat, so they do not affect the fat or calorie content of hash browns

   instant versus quick, or old-fashioned cooking: the time necessary for cooking grits does not affect its fat content

the fattiest . . .

food (one-cup serving)	cals	fat (g)	fat (%)	sat (g)	sodium (mg)
corned beef hash	360-420	20-28	47-60	8-10	855-1545
roast beef hash	355	23	59	8	745

The very high fat content of **corned beef and roast beef hash** is probably the reason manufacturers have in the past seldom listed its nutrition information on their labels. Now that the new labeling law prevents most manufacturers from withholding this information, it will be interesting to see if they feel the pressure to lower the high fat content of hash.

the less fatty . . .

food (70 grams, or half-cup serving)	cals	fat (g)	fat (%)	sat (g)	sodium (mg)
deep-fried hash brown potatoes	170-205	9-14	48-63	3-5	300-495

Deep-fried hash brown potatoes, the kind sold in fast-food restaurants, tend to absorb more fat than more intact or "whole" forms of potatoes, such as home fries or French fries. There are two reasons for this. First, shredding exposes more of the potato's surface area to the cooking fat. Second, the complete immersion in cooking oil exposes more of the potato to this fat.

the leaner . . .

food (70 grams, or half-cup serving)	cals	fat (g)	fat (%)	sat (g)	sodium (mg)
hash browns prepared from frozen potatoes					
oil is already included microwave-heated	140	8	49	1	150
toasted in toaster	140	7	45	1	325
broiled	130	7	48	1	205
you supply the oil fried	100-155	5-8	47-50	0-3	25-30
other hash browns products for which you supply the oil					
fried from refrigerated potatoes	125-135	6	41-45	0	60-270
fried from dehydrated mix	135-145	5	34-36	0	415-465

All these products are similar in their fat content. Brands of
frozen hash browns include Ore-Ida and Aunt Jemima.
Refrigerated hash browns are made by Simply Potatoes.
Betty Crocker makes **dehydrated hash potato mixes.**

TIP: Don't be fooled by the nutrition labels. Some of these
packages list the fat content *before* the potatoes are cooked in
the oil that the directions instruct you to use.

the leanest . . .

food (one-cup serving)	cals	fat (g)	fat (%)	sat (g)	sodium (mg)
grits					
flavored with ham/butter/cheese	180-200	2-4	9-18	0	700-1240
plain	160-200	0	0	0	0-540

Grits, or coarsely ground corn, is usually the leanest of the hot side dishes people eat with breakfast—at least until butter is added.

fat-skimming tips:
- skip the hash

- use gravy instead of butter on grits because most gravies have far less fat than butter or margarine

see these pages for:
224 catsup
228 gravies
203 butter or margarine
126 french fries

cals=calories; fat=grams of fat; %fat=percent of calories from fat; sat=grams of saturated fat; sodium=milligrams of sodium

Breakfast Sandwiches

Breakfast sandwiches have become one of today's most popular foods for breakfast. Not surprisingly, because of their origin in fast-food restaurants, they can be one of the fattiest breakfasts available if you're not careful.

things that affect the fat content:
choice of the sandwich's outside: in general, croissants are fattier than biscuits, and biscuits are fattier than bagels, English muffins, or tortillas.

choice of the inside: in general, sausage is fattier than bacon, bacon is fattier than beef, beef is fattier than ham, and ham is fattier than Canadian bacon, eggs, or imitation meat

multiple ingredients: combinations of meats, eggs, and cheese will, naturally, provide more fat than just one of these fillings.

TIP: To identify the fattiest breakfast sandwiches, look for croissants or biscuits with sausage inside, perhaps with an additional egg or slice of cheese. For the leanest, look for bagels or English muffins wrapped around Canadian bacon or eggs.

the fattiest . . .

food (one)	cals	fat (g)	fat (%)	sat (g)	chol (mg)	sodium (mg)
sandwiches with pork sausage						
croissant	520-585	38-43	66-68	13-19	185-270	630-1115
biscuit	350-580	21-39	48-63	7-15	35-300	780-1310
bagel	625	36	52	12	295	1135
English muffin	345-485	20-31	52-57	7-12	55-275	770-1135
sandwiches with bacon						
croissant	360-415	24-28	60-62	8-15	215-225	580-890
biscuit	320-475	18-31	45-61	4-11	10-355	865-1260
bagel	345	20	40	7	250	870

food (one)	cals	fat (g)	fat (%)	sat (g)	chol (mg)	sodium (mg)
sandwiches with steak						
biscuit	330-550	15-32	41-54	7-9	25-270	795-1370
English muffin	360	20	50	—	—	730

Restaurants offering these and other sandwiches include McDonald's, Burger King, Arby's, Wendy's, Jack in the Box, and Hardee's. Brands of frozen sandwiches in the supermarket include Swanson's Great Starts, Hormel, Morningstar Farms, Weight Watchers, and Healthy Choice.

the less fatty . . .

food (one)	cals	fat (g)	fat (%)	sat (g)	chol (mg)	sodium (mg)
sandwiches with ham						
croissant	345-475	21-34	55-64	7-17	90-240	940-1080
biscuit	320-440	16-27	43-55	2-11	15-300	1000-1600
bagel	240-440	8-17	30-35	6	265	600-1115

the leaner . . .

food (one)	cals	fat (g)	fat (%)	sat (g)	chol (mg)	sodium (mg)
sandwiches with Canadian bacon						
biscuit	420-470	22-27	47-52	8	180	1550-1845
English muffin	250-385	8-20	29-46	4-9	115-235	680-1110
sandwiches with eggs						
croissant	315-370	20-25	57-60	7-14	215-220	550-605
biscuit	315	20	58	6	230	655
bagel	405	16	35	5	245	760

the leanest . . .

food (one)	cals	fat (g)	fat (%)	sat (g)	chol (mg)	sodium (mg)
McDonald's breakfast burrito	280	17	55	4	135	580
sandwiches with imitation meats	280-370	11-17	35-41	2-3	0	570-780
Swanson's breakfast burritos	200-250	7-13	32-47	—	—	500-540
McDonald's Egg McMuffin	280	11	35	4	235	710
"lite" sandwiches						
Weight Watchers brand	180-230	5-11	25-45	2-4	10-160	410-590
Healthy Choice brand	200-210	3-4	14-17	2	15-20	470-480

McDonald's Egg McMuffin is an example of how to construct a leaner breakfast sandwich: it's made with an English muffin instead of a biscuit or croissant, and it contains Canadian bacon instead of sausage. However, it does contain, in addition to that, an egg and cheese—and that's what makes it higher in fat than the leanest sandwiches available.

Sandwiches containing imitation meats, which are manufactured from soybeans, are available from Morningstar Farms. Weight Watchers' and Healthy Choice's sandwiches are English muffins with ham, Canadian bacon, and egg substitutes.

cals=calories; fat=grams of fat; %fat=percent of calories from fat; sat=grams of saturated fat; sodium=milligrams of sodium

sweets

Breakfast Pastry to Be Heated

The appeal of a sweet food in the morning seems to be universal. It's easy to satisfy the craving with these ready-to-heat pastries, so be aware of what is in them.

things that affect the fat content:
flakiness: this is usually the result of butter and shortening, so a flaky pastry like turnovers will usually have more fat than rolls or cake

presence of cheese: cheese will raise the fat level

use of streusel icing: this adds more fat and calories

the fattiest . . .

food (one serving)	cals	fat (g)	fat (%)	sat (g)	sodium (mg)
higher-fat fruit or cheese turnovers	300-310	17-19	49-55	5-6	210-280

Pepperidge Farm is a national brand of **higher-fat turnovers.**

the less fatty . . .

food (one serving)	cals	fat (g)	fat (%)	sat (g)	sodium (mg)
higher-fat frozen cinnamon rolls	280-290	11-14	34-45	2-3	190-220
frozen Danish	220-250	8-14	33-53	3-5	130-230
frozen streusel coffee cake	230	11-12	43-47	2	240

The brands of **higher-fat cinnamon rolls** include Pepperidge Farm and Sara Lee. The **frozen Danish** is available from Pepperidge Farm, the **streusel coffee cake** from Pillsbury.

the leaner . . .

food (one serving)	cals	fat (g)	fat (%)	sat (g)	sodium (mg)
frozen pastry					
croissants	170	7-9	37-48	2	240-250
streudel toaster pastry	180-190	7-9	35-43	2	180-210
sweet rolls	160-190	7-8	33-45	1-2	240-250
coffee cake	160	7	39		160
"petite" croissant	120	6	45	1	160
lower-fat cinnamon rolls	160-180	4-5	23-25	1	170-190
refrigerated dough					
turnovers	170	8	42	2	330
Danish dough	150	7	42	2	230-250
cinnamon roll dough	110-150	5-7	32-42	1-2	260-320
medium-fat toaster pastries	190-210	5-7	21-30	1-2	115-220

Frozen croissants are available from Sara Lee and Pepperidge Farm. Pillsbury's **frozen streudel toaster pastry** is one of the fattiest toaster pastries. Pillsbury and Weight Watchers are two brands of **frozen sweet rolls. Frozen coffee cake** and **petite croissants** are sold by Sara Lee. And Weight Watchers makes **lower-fat frozen cinnamon rolls.** Pillsbury is a major brand of refrigerated dough for making **turnovers, Danish,** and **cinnamon rolls.** Note that pastry made from refrigerated dough has less fat than frozen pastries.

Medium-fat toaster pastries include the Pastry Poppers, Toast 'Em, Toastettes, and Kellogg's Pop-Tarts brands.

the leanest . . .

food (one serving)	cals	fat (g)	fat (%)	sat (g)	sodium (mg)
low-fat toaster pastry	155-165	1	3	0	160-190
fat-free frozen sweet rolls	180	0		0	0	230

A **low-fat toaster pastry** brand is Toast 'n Jammers. **Fat-free sweet rolls** are made by Mrs. Butterworth's.

fat-skimming tips:

  • toaster pastries are among the leanest breakfast pastries

  • Pepperidge Farm and Sara Lee products are frequently among the higher-fat

see these pages for:
    37 fast-food breakfast pastries
    181 snack cakes

cals=calories; fat=grams of fat; %fat=percent of calories from fat; sat=grams of saturated fat; sodium=milligrams of sodium

Instant Breakfasts: Bars and Milk Mixes

The most common reason people give for not eating breakfast is the lack of time in the morning to sit down and eat a prepared meal. It's no wonder that "instant" meals consisting of powders to mix into milk, or bars to rip open on the way out the door, are popular.

things that affect the fat content:
flavoring with nuts, peanut butter, or chocolate in the breakfast bars: this generally means more fat than you'll get in the fruit-flavored and oat bran selections of the same brand

the kind of milk used to make the beverages: whether the milk is whole, low-fat, or skim affects the fat content of instant breakfast beverages more than anything else

flavoring with chocolate in the beverages: chocolate-flavored beverages often contain slightly more fat than the vanilla- or strawberry-flavored ones

the fattiest . . .

food (one serving)	cals	fat (g)	fat (%)	sat (g)	sodium (mg)
higher-fat granola bars	195-220	11-14	48-59	6-8	60-90
chocolate- or fudge-coated granola bars	185-215	9-13	45-55	7	60-90
breakfast bars	140	4-6	26-39	2-3	65

The fattiest instant breakfasts are the granola-type products sold as **breakfast bars,** usually in the same supermarket aisle as breakfast cereals. Nearly all of them contain more fat than most cereals. In fact, they're similar to candy bars (see the section on candy bars). **Granola bars** are described in more detail in the section on snack bars.

the less fatty . . .

food (one bar or one cup/8 fluid oz.)	cals	fat (g)	fat (%)	sat (g)	sodium (mg)
most granola bars	140-200	6-10	28-46	1-7	20-170
beverage prepared from regular instant breakfast powder					
with whole milk	280	8-10	26-32	5	220-330
with 2% milk	250	5-7	18-25	3	220-330

The fat in these **instant breakfast beverages** is derived almost entirely from the milk, so the choice of which milk to mix the powder into is most important. The chocolate flavors will have more fat, the fruit or vanilla flavors less fat.

the leanest . . .

food (one cup/8 fluid oz.)	cals	fat (g)	fat (%)	sat (g)	sodium (mg)
beverage prepared from regular instant breakfast powder					
with 1% milk	230	3-5	12-20	2	225-335
with skim milk	215	0-2	0-8	0	225-335
beverage prepared from "lite" instant breakfast powder					
with skim milk	155	0-2	0-12	0	240-260

Again, most of this fat is contributed by the milk. The chocolate flavors will have more fat, the fruit or vanilla flavors less fat. Carnation makes a "lite" form of instant breakfast which is sweetened with aspartame in place of sugar.

fat-skimming tips:

- choose your granola bar carefully because there are wide differences in their fat content (see the section on snack bars)
- use the leanest milk you can for instant breakfast beverages

see these pages for:
238 milks
164 snack bars

cals=calories; fat=grams of fat; %fat=percent of calories from fat; sat=grams of saturated fat; sodium=milligrams of sodium

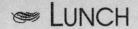 LUNCH

sandwich breads and fillings
sandwich bread, rolls, and buns
sandwich spreads: peanut butter, jelly, tuna fish
luncheon meats: bologna, salami, meat spreads
sandwich meats: ham, chicken, turkey, and beef
hot dogs, frankfurters, knocks, and weiners
canned fish: tuna, salmon, sardines, shellfish

salads and soups
prepared lettuce salads: chef, garden, side, taco
salad bar choices
soups: ramen, noodle, rice, barley
soups: meat, seafood, cheese
soups: vegetable
soups: bean, pea, lentil

dairy foods
yogurt and cottage cheese
hard, natural cheeses
process cheeses

restaurant lunches
hamburgers and cheeseburgers
hot dogs and buns
chicken sandwiches
beef sandwiches
fish fillet sandwiches
french fries, baked potatoes, and hush puppies

sandwich breads and fillings

Sandwich Bread, Rolls, and Buns
Most breads and sandwich rolls are low in fat, so these are not likely to be a significant source of fat in a sandwich. What's put in or on them matters most.

this affects the fat or calorie content:
size of the roll or bun: size makes the most difference—the bigger the bun, the greater the fat and calories

things that do not affect the fat or calorie content:
- the source of the grain or starch: wheat, potato, or rye breads of similar size all have about the same number of calories

- club versus kaiser, hard, or other rolls: there are no significant differences among them

- using hamburger or hot dog buns: these are similar to sandwich breads in their fat and calories

the fattiest . . .

food (one)	cals	fat (g)	fat (%)	sat (g)	sodium (mg)
submarine or hoagie rolls	210-240	3-5	13-21	0-1	260-320

At 6 to 8 inches in length, these are the biggest rolls and, thus, contain the most fat and calories.

the other choices . . .

food (one roll or two slices)	cals	fat (g)	fat (%)	sat (g)	sodium (mg)
hot dog or hamburger rolls	100-140	1-3	6-19	0-1	130-280
most sandwich breads (2 slices)	130-140	2	13-14	0-1	130-300
sandwich rolls large (about 2.5 oz)	180-190	1-2	5-9	0	340-415
medium (about 2 oz)	105-180	0-3	6-18	0-1	195-400
small (about 1.5 oz)	90-140	1-3	5-30	0-2	75-270
"lite" sandwich buns	80	1-2	11-23	0	190-210
pita or pocket bread	110-160	0-1	0-8	0	0-310

Sandwich breads are discussed in more detail in the section on breads for breakfast. **"Lite" sandwich buns,** such as Wonder brand, are prepared with extra fiber, which replaces some of the starch and its calories. Overall, **pita, or pocket, bread** is likely to contain the least amount of fat. It usually consists of just flour, water, and salt.

fat-skimming tips:
- far more significant than the choice of bread is the choice of what to put in or on it
- pita bread is often the choice with the very least fat

see this page for:
9 breads and bagels

cals=calories; fat=grams of fat; %fat=percent of calories from fat; sat=grams of saturated fat; sodium=milligrams of sodium

Sandwich Spreads: Peanut Butter, Jelly, Tuna Fish

Americans have been filling their sandwiches with peanut butter, jelly, tuna fish, and other spreads for generations. Of these three, nut butters, unfortunately, are a very fatty food. Today, several new, leaner alternatives to regular peanut butter are beginning to become available.

this affects the fat content:

whipping peanut butter: new peanut butters that have been whipped with air take up more space, so a spoonful will contain about 20 percent less peanut butter and, thus, 20 percent less fat.

things that do not affect the fat content:

the type of nut or seed used to make butter: the differences in fat among nuts and seeds are minor and, as a result, so are the differences in fat among their butters

chunky versus smooth style peanut butter: both kinds contain the same amount of fat and calories

old-fashioned or natural style versus regular peanut butter: regular peanut butters have hydrogenated fat added to help them spread more easily, whereas old-fashioned or natural peanut butters do not. But this does not significantly affect the fat content because peanut butter consists of mostly fat, whether this is the fat found naturally in peanuts or the vegetable oil added to it.

the fattiest . . .

food (2 tablespoons)	cals	fat (g)	fat (%)	sat (g)	sodium (mg)
sesame butter or tahini	195-220	19	78-90	2	0-5
almond butter	190-210	17-18	78-81	2	5
peanut butter	180-190	16-17	76-81	2-3	0-155
cashew butter	190	16	76	3	5

All of these nut butters have similar amounts of fat. The composition of peanut butter is established by federal law, so only trivial nutritional differences exist among brands.

the less fatty . . .

food (2 tablespoons)	cals	fat (g)	fat (%)	sat (g)	sodium (mg)
whipped peanut butter	140-160	12-14	76-79	1-2	10-110
reduced-fat peanut butter	190	12	57	2	140
mayonnaise-based sandwich spread	100	10	90	2	190
hazelnut-cocoa spread	170	10	53		10
brand-name peanut butter and jelly	150-180	7-10	42-50	1-2	55-120
homemade peanut butter and jelly	140-145	8-9	48-55	1-2	0-80

Peanut butter whipped with air has about 20 percent less fat per serving. Peter Pan and Crazy Richard's are two such brands. Peter Pan's Smart Choice is a reduced-fat peanut butter in which soybean protein has replaced some of the nuts. Kraft makes a sandwich spread that is essentially mayonnaise and relish. Nutella is a hazelnut and cocoa spread popular in Italy and now available here in many supermarkets. Since jelly is fat-free, a mixture of half peanut butter and half jelly cuts the fat of peanut butter in half; Smucker's Goober is one national brand.

the leaner . . .

food (4 tablespoons or 2 oz.)	cals	fat (g)	fat (%)	sat (g)	sodium (mg)
homemade tuna salad	95-100	5-6	45-57	1	145-290
brand-name prepared tuna salad	80	5	56	1	220

Homemade tuna salad here is based on a typical recipe using mayonnaise. Libby's is a brand of prepared tuna salad for sandwiches.

the leanest . . .

food (one tablespoon)	cals	fat (g)	fat (%)	sat (g)	sodium (mg)
jam, jelly, preserves, or marmalade	50-55	0	0	0	5-10

Plain jam, jelly, preserves, and marmalade are the leanest and lightest food to spread on bread.

fat-skimming tips:
 • look for reduced-fat or whipped peanut butter

• replace mayonnaise with mustard

see these pages for:
187 cheese spreads
60 canned fish

cals=calories; fat=grams of fat; %fat=percent of calories from fat; sat=grams of
saturated fat; sodium=milligrams of sodium

Luncheon Meats: Bologna, Salami, Meat Spreads

Luncheon meats like bologna or salami are a traditional way of
using and preserving fattier cuts of meat. Today, this form of
preservation is no longer necessary, but luncheon meats con-
tinue to be popular for their taste and, in some cases, for their
apparently lower cost. Unfortunately, many consist of more fat
than meat, along with a wallop of sodium. Cold cuts of ham,
beef, chicken, and turkey are discussed in another section.

things that affect the fat content:
use of liver: meats made from the liver, such as liver sausage
and liver cheese, tend to have more fat than other meats

use of turkey or chicken in place of beef or pork: because
poultry is leaner than beef or pork and because adding too
much fat to them ruins their taste, luncheon meats made from
poultry will usually contain less fat

this doesn't affect the fat content:
choice of pork or beef or a combination of the two: pork and
beef are similar enough in fat content so that their relative
amounts make little difference in these processed meats. A
combination of the two is often labeled "meat."

the fattiest . . .

food (55 grams or 2 oz.)	cals	fat (g)	fat (%)	sat (g)	sodium (mg)
liver sausage (braunschweiger)	155-200	12-18	68-82	6	480-650
deviled ham spread	140-200	12-17	74-78	5-7	
higher-fat bologna	170-180	15-17	80-83	6-7	475-610
sandwich steaks	170-180	15-16	79-80	6-8	80
Spam brand luncheon meat	170	16	84	6	740
summer sausage	165	15	78	6	770-780
liver cheese	170	14-15	76-78	5	605-680
mortadella	175	14	74	5	695

Underwood and Hormel make canned deviled ham spread. Higher-fat bologna, such as Oscar Mayer and Smok-A-Roma brands, has about the same composition as hot dogs. Frozen sandwich steaks, such as Steak-Umm brand, are fabricated from fatty cuts of beef. Spam is chopped pork shoulder meat with ham added. Liver cheese is made from pork livers.

the less fatty . . .

food (55 grams or 2 oz.)	cals	fat (g)	fat (%)	sat (g)	sodium (mg)
cooked salami: beef, pork, or meat	110-155	9-14	69-79	3-5	610-710
reduced-fat Spam brand luncheon meat	140	12	77	4	550
medium-fat bologna made with chicken or turkey	120-140	10-12	75-77	3-4	470-650

food (55 grams or 2 oz.)	cals	fat (g)	fat (%)	sat (g)	sodium (mg)
80% fat-free by weight	140	11	72	4	600
ham & cheese/pickle & pimiento/olive loaf	125-145	8-11	56-73	3-5	650-775
roast beef or chicken spreads	120-140	8-10	54-71	3-4	
potted meat	100-120	8-10	60-74	3-4	

Cooked salami is usually leaner than bologna. Regular bologna is about 70% fat-free by weight, so 80% fat-free bologna contains about one-third less fat.

the leaner . . .

food (55 grams or 2 oz.)	cals	fat (g)	fat (%)	sat (g)	sodium (mg)
picnic, luncheon, olive, old-fashioned loaves	120-130	8-9	59-64	3	645-825
headcheese	95-120	7-9	64-67	3	690-700
turkey luncheon meats: summer sausage, salami, luncheon loaf	90-110	6-8	60-65	2-3	520-670
lebanon bologna	105-125	5-8	45-59	2-3	705-720
reduced-fat canned meat spreads	85-110	5-7	45-60	2-3	
reduced-fat liver sausage	110-120	6-8	49-58	3	400-530
lower-fat, 90% fat-free bologna	60-90	5-6	60-75	2-3	425-570
prepared turkey, chicken, or ham salads	70-100	3-6	39-60	1	230-380
New England sausage	70-100	3-6	40-54	1	680-690

Lebanon bologna is a fermented luncheon meat lower in fat than conventional bologna. Underwood is a brand of reduced-fat canned meat spreads. Jones Dairy Farm and Russer Lil' Salt are brands of reduced-fat liver sausage. Hillshire Farm, Louis Rich, and Hebrew National are brands of 90% fat-free bologna.

the leanest . . .

food (55 grams or 2 oz.)	cals	fat (g)	fat (%)	sat (g)	sodium (mg)
honey loaf	65-70	2	25-32	1	735-745
97% fat-free bologna	55-90	1-2	10-30	0-1	370-665

Honey loaf is made from meat, honey, and dried milk, and is one of the leanest luncheon meats available. Healthy Choice, Tyson's, and Oscar Mayer's Healthy Favorites are brands of very low-fat, 97% fat-free bologna.

see these pages for:
  53 cold cuts of ham, beef, chicken, and turkey
  50 meat spreads for sandwiches

cals=calories; fat=grams of fat; %fat=percent of calories from fat; sat=grams of saturated fat; sodium=milligrams of sodium

Sandwich Meats: Ham, Chicken, Turkey, and Beef

Lean slices of ham, chicken, turkey, and beef are now easily available for making low-fat sandwiches. These are now among the leanest fillings you can choose. Luncheon meats such as bologna and salami, which are considerably fattier, are examined in another section.

this affects the fat content:
chopping and pressing to form meat slices: slices of luncheon meat which have been formed from pieces of chopped and pressed meat are fattier than whole, intact slices because fattier cuts are used in this process.

things that do not affect the fat content:
source of meat: ham, chicken, turkey, and beef are all now available in lean selections

roasting versus baking versus boiling: cooking methods do not affect the fat content

the fattiest . . .

food (55 grams or 2 oz.)	cals	fat (g)	fat (%)	sat (g)	sodium (mg)
chopped ham	100-145	7-12	60-77	3-4	635-800

This is usually the fattiest form of ham you can buy. Examples of brands are Oscar Mayer, Hormel Black Label, and Smok-A-Roma.

the less fatty . . .

food (55 grams or 2 oz.)	cals	fat (g)	fat (%)	sat (g)	sodium (mg)
pressed and formed meats	80-120	4-8	45-63	2-4	640-860
chicken or turkey roll	85	4	42-44	1	275-325

These have been formed into slices from pieces of meat. They can include beef, chicken, pastrami, corned beef, turkey, and ham. Examples of brands are Buddig, Smok-A-Roma, and Weaver.

the leaner . . .

food (55 grams or 2 oz.)	cals	fat (g)	fat (%)	sat (g)	sodium (mg)
turkey ham	50-80	2-4	26-51	1	500-650

Turkey ham is cured dark meat. Since dark meat contains more fat than white meat, this has more fat than slices of turkey breast.

the leanest . . .

food (55 grams or 2 oz.)	cals	fat (g)	fat (%)	sat (g)	sodium (mg)
pastrami or corned beef	50-70	1-3	18-36	1	400-625
turkey breast	50-70	1-2	8-30	0-1	35-805
roast beef	50-70	1-2	18-29	0-1	430-855
chicken breast	50-70	1-2	7-36	0	450-725
lean ham	50-65	1-2	17-31	0-1	450-870

All of these lean sandwich meats are now widely available. Look for those at least 95 percent fat-free, with the leanest 98 or 99 percent fat-free. Brands include Hebrew National, Oscar Mayer, Louis Rich, Butterball, Land O' Frost, Healthy Choice, Hillshire Farm Deli Select, and Mr. Turkey.

fat-skimming tips:
   • look for the turkey alternatives, such as turkey pastrami or ham

see this page for:
   50 bologna

cals=calories; fat=grams of fat; %fat=percent of calories from fat; sat=grams of saturated fat; sodium=milligrams of sodium

Hot Dogs, Frankfurters, Knocks, and Weiners

Whether you call them hot dogs, frankfurters, red hots, knocks, or weiners, they're all the same—one of America's favorite foods but a major source of fat in the national diet.

things that affect the fat content:
size of the sausage: hot dogs are available in sizes ranging from 1.2 ounces to 4 ounces, so naturally the size makes a very big difference in the fat content

use of chicken or turkey meat: products made with these meats will contain less fat, ounce for ounce, than those made with beef or pork—but these poultry franks can still contain large amounts of fat

percentage of fat: here's a chart to help interpret the percent fat-free claims on labels:

Grams of Fat for Each Size of Frank and Fat-Free Percent

percent fat-free	2 oz.	1.6 oz.	1.2 oz.
80	11	9	7
85	9	7	5
90	6	5	3
95	3	2	2
97	2	1	1

things that do not affect the fat content:
choice of beef or pork: these meats are similar enough in their fat content that which one you choose makes little difference.

Those made from a combination of beef and pork are called "meat" sausages

smokie, knocks, or knockwurst varieties: these are coarser in texture and may contain spicy or smoky flavorings, but they contain the same amount of fat as other sausages of an equivalent size

kosher processing: kosher franks have the same fat content as non-kosher franks

the fattiest . . .

food (one, 4 oz.)	cals	fat (g)	fat (%)	sat (g)	sodium (mg)
jumbo or quarter-pound franks	350-360	32-34	85	13-14	1165-1190
Polish/German sausage or knockwurst	350	32	82	13	1250

Quarter-pound, 4-ounce frankfurters or **sausages** are among the fattiest meats you can buy. And they pack a lot of sodium.

the less fatty . . .

food (one)	cals	fat (g)	fat (%)	sat (g)	sodium (mg)
large (2 ounces, or 8 to a pound)					
meat, beef, or smokie	170-190	14-17	74-85	7	470-600
chicken, 22-25% fat by weight	150-160	13-14	71-83	4	380-675
chicken, 16-20% fat by weight	120-140	9-11	68-76	3	380-650

food (one)	cals	fat (g)	fat (%)	sat (g)	sodium (mg)
turkey, 18-20% fat by weight	130-140	10-11	69-76	3	650
80-85% fat-free meat franks by weight	130-150	11-12	72-76	5	530-635
medium (1.6 ounces, or 10 to a pound)					
meat or beef	130-150	12-14	78-84	6	410-500
smokie	125-130	11-12	80-83	4-5	425-500
small (1.2 ounces, or 10 to a 12-oz. package)					
beef	110	10	82	4	350

Hot dogs are permitted by federal law to contain up to 30 percent of their weight in fat. The percentage of fat in chicken or turkey franks can vary from 14 to 25 percent by weight, so it pays to read the labels to identify those with a lower percentage of fat.

the leaner . . .

food (one)	cals	fat (g)	fat (%)	sat (g)	sodium (mg)
large (2 oz.)					
turkey, 14% fat by weight	110	8	65	2	250
90% fat-free meat/beef franks	90	5	50	2	510
medium (1.6 oz.)					
chicken	110	9	74	3	305-585
turkey	105-110	9	74-76	3	440-450
higher-fat vegetarian franks	70-120	4-9	47-68	1	160-440

small (1.2 oz.)					
turkey	80	7	79	2	390
chicken	70-80	6-7	77-79	2	390
higher-fat vegetarian franks	70-85	5-7	64-69	2	165-170

Vegetarian franks are made from soybeans. Brands include Worthington Foods, Soy Boy's Not Dogs, and Lightlife's Tofu Pups.

the leanest . . .

food (one)	cals	fat (g)	fat (%)	sat (g)	sodium (mg)
97% fat-free franks	50-65	1-2	28	0-1	460-525
fat-free vegetarian franks	40	0	0	0	290

Healthy Choice and Oscar Mayer are brands of **97 percent fat-free franks** made from meat and milk ingredients. Lightlife's Smart Dogs are a **fat-free vegetarian frank** made from soybeans.

fat-skimming tips:
- choose 97 percent fat-free franks—you can save 10–15 grams of fat with each one

- try vegetarian franks

see these pages for
  91 hot dog buns
  226 mustard
  224 catsup
  231 relish

cals=calories; fat=grams of fat; %fat=percent of calories from fat; sat=grams of saturated fat; sodium=milligrams of sodium

Canned Fish: Tuna, Salmon, Sardines, Shellfish

Canned fish can be a wholesome, low-fat food to eat—if you know what to look for and what to avoid. Those canned with their bones are also excellent sources of calcium.

things that affect the fat content:
packing medium: most important is what the fish is canned in—fish packed in oil will naturally contain more fat than fish packed in tomato sauce, mustard sauce, or water, especially if the oil is not drained off

sardines versus tuna or salmon: sardines are an oilier fish than tuna or salmon, so they will have more fat

type of salmon: canned sockeye salmon usually contains more fat than canned pink salmon

presence of skin on fish: salmon with the skin has more fat than salmon without the skin

things that do not affect the fat content:
white versus light type of tuna: there is no difference in fat content

chunk versus flaked style: this doesn't affect the fat

type of oil used in canning: the oils used are similar in composition

mustard versus tomato, or hot sauce: all of these are low-calorie, low-fat sauces for canning fish

the fattiest . . .

food (55 grams or 2 oz.)	cals	fat (g)	fat (%)	sat (g)	sodium (mg)
sardines in oil, without draining oil	240	22	82	3	60-235

Sardines packed in oil have twice as much fat if the oil has not been drained off before eating.

the less fatty . . .

food (55 grams or 2 oz.)	cals	fat (g)	fat (%)	sat (g)	sodium (mg)
tuna in oil, without draining oil	135-155	10-13	64-78	2	245-305
sardines in oil, with oil drained	135-150	10-12	69-70	1-2	60-260

Tuna packed in oil that has not been drained off will contain twice as much fat as tuna with its oil removed.

the leaner . . .

food (55 grams or 2 oz.)	cals	fat (g)	fat (%)	sat (g)	sodium (mg)
sardines packed in water or sauce	85-125	7-9	60-68	2	60-335
kippers	90-120	5-7	48-51	2	330-505
salmon, sockeye	85-100	4-6	43-50	1	260-295
tuna in oil, with oil drained	100-110	4-5	37-39	1	195-215
salmon, pink, with skin	70-90	3-4	36-45	1	220-270
mackerel	70-85	3-4	36-51	1	210-235

Sardines packed in tomato or mustard sauce contain about the same amount of calories and fat as those packed in water. **Kippers** are smoked or smoke-flavored herring. **Salmon with the skin on** contains 1 to 2 grams more fat than salmon with the skin removed.

the leanest . . .

food (55 grams or 2 oz.)	cals	fat (g)	fat (%)	sat (g)	sodium (mg)
salmon, pink, skinless	60-70	2-3	30-38	0	230-275
tuna packed in water	50-75	1-2	12-26	0	55-305
oysters	40-55	1-2	33-36	0	125-215
clams, shrimp, crab	55-80	1	11-15	0	95-345

Tuna and shellfish packed in water are among the leanest and lightest protein foods you can buy.

fat-skimming tips:
- look for fish canned in water, mustard sauce, tomato sauce, or hot sauce

- drain the oil from canned fish to cut its fat in half

- for tunafish salad, try a reduced-fat or fat-free mayonnaise or salad dressing

see these pages for:
118 fish
118 shellfish
209 mayonnaise and salad dressing

cals=calories; fat=grams of fat; %fat=percent of calories from fat; sat=grams of saturated fat; sodium=milligrams of sodium

salads and soups

Prepared Lettuce Salads:
Chef, Garden, Side, Taco

Almost all restaurants, even fast-food ones, now offer some kind of salad on their menus. The fat content of these ranges from nothing to astronomical, so it's worth knowing what to avoid.

things that affect the fat content:
taco salad shells: the edible shell served with some taco salads can contain 30 grams of fat

the amount of cheese and eggs: in most salads, the amount of these ingredients has the most impact on the fat content

ground meat versus cold cuts: ground meat is much fattier than cold cuts of beef, ham, chicken, or turkey, so salads made with ground beef, such as taco salads, will contain more fat than those made with cold cuts

this doesn't affect the fat content:
the type of lettuce and vegetables: these all contribute few calories and virtually no fat to salads

NOTE: As with all salads, the dressing is critical to the fat content. The following salads are listed *without* salad dressing.

the fattiest . . .

food (one)	cals	fat (g)	fat (%)	sat (g)	chol	sodium (mg)
taco salad with shell	905	61	61	19	80	910
taco salad without the shell	485-660	31-37	50-58	14-17	35-90	680-1600

Taco salads, such as those served by Taco Bell, are the fattiest of the salads because they can consist of ground beef, cheese, and sour cream served inside a fried tortilla shell.

the less fatty . . .

food (one)	cals	fat (g)	fat (%)	sat (g)	chol	sodium (mg)
chef salads	170-325	9-18	45-56	4-8	0-170	140-930
garden salads with lots of cheese and eggs	200-210	13-14	59-60	8	100-185	240-270

The fat in **chef salads** is contributed by the eggs, cheese, and meat it contains. **Garden salads** that omit the meat can have just as much fat, depending upon the amount of cheese and eggs.

the leaner . . .

food (one)	cals	fat (g)	fat (%)	sat (g)	chol	sodium (mg)
seafood salads	110-230	5-12	20-57	1-2	90	455-945
beef, ham, turkey salads	165-185	9-10	49-53	2-5	75	480
chicken salads	125-200	4-8	24-58	1-4	30-80	230-560

These **meat and seafood salads** contain lesser amounts of fat because the meats in them are leaner than cheese and eggs.

the leanest . . .

food (one)	cals	fat (g)	fat (%)	sat (g)	chol	sodium (mg)
garden salads with little or no eggs and cheese	45-110	0-5	0-54	0-3	0-65	60-635
side salads	10-50	0-3	0-53	0	0-35	5-85

These **garden and side salads** consist mostly of low-calorie, low-fat vegetables such as lettuce, tomatoes, and cucumbers.

fat-skimming tips:
- with all salads, the dressing can be the source of most of the fat

- in most salads, the cheese, eggs, and sometimes the meat contribute the most fat and calories

- don't eat the shell of a taco salad

see this page for:
    211 salad dressings

cals=calories; fat=grams of fat; %fat=percent of calories from fat; sat=grams of saturated fat; sodium=milligrams of sodium

Salad Bar Choices

the fattiest . . .

food (one serving)	cals	fat (%)	fat (g)	sat (mg)	sodium
shredded cheese (2 tablespoons)	55-65	4-5	68-74	3	85-300
cottage cheese (half-cup)	95-145	1-5	9-41	1-3	175-495
sunflower seeds (1 tablespoon)	45	4	80	1	40
olives (6-8)	30-35	3-4	77-100	0	220-720

food (one serving)	cals	fat (g)	fat (%)	sat (g)	sodium
croutons (one-third cup)	50-70	2-4	18-45	0-2	100-200
beans (half-cup)	120-160	0-4	0-23	0	385-480

the less fatty . . .

food (one serving)	cals	fat (g)	fat (%)	sat (g)	sodium (mg)
eggs (2 tablespoons)	40	3	68	1	30-135
bacon or imitation bacon (1 tablespoon)	20-35	1-3	25-66	0-1	90-250
diced meat (2 tablespoons)	30	1-3	30-90	0-1	95-210

the leaner . . .

food (one serving)	cals	fat (g)	fat (%)	sat (g)	sodium (mg)
chow mein noodles (2 tablespoons)	35-40	2	45-51	0	55-90
Parmesan cheese (1 tablespoon)	20-25	2	59	1	80-95
bean salad (half-cup)	90-130	0-2	0-14	0	10-35
green peas (half-cup)	70	1	13	0	340

the leanest . . .

food (one serving)	cals	fat (g)	fat (%)	sat (g)	sodium (mg)
fruit (half-cup)	30-95	0	0	0	0-25
lettuce and vegetables (half-cup)	10-40	0	0	0	0-300

food (one serving)	cals (g)	fat (%)	fat (g)	sat (mg)	sodium
pickles, peppers, radishes (2 tablespoons)	0-5	0	0	0	5-400

cals=calories; fat=grams of fat; %fat=percent of calories from fat; sat=grams of saturated fat; sodium=milligrams of sodium

Soups: Ramen, Noodle, Rice, Barley

Ramen soups have become popular as inexpensive, filling, and simple dishes to prepare either at home or away from home. Unfortunately, they are the saltiest and can be among the fattiest soups available. Since grains are low in fat to begin with, most of the fat in these soups is contributed by other ingredients.

things that affect the fat content:
use of fried ramen noodles: some ramen noodles are fried during their manufacturing, so soups made with these noodles contain more fat than soups made with rice or pasta—but there are low-fat ramen soups available now

cups versus blocks of ramen noodle soup: cups to which hot water is added usually contain more fat than the blocks of noodles, which are boiled and then mixed with a flavoring powder

chunky versus regular soups: thicker, denser soups usually contain more fat and calories

this doesn't affect the fat content:
source of meat or seafood: since only small amounts of lean meat or seafood are used in these soups, the presence of these ingredients does not significantly raise the fat content

the fattiest . . .

food (one cup serving)	cals	fat (g)	fat (%)	sat (g)	sodium (mg)
ramen noodle soups in cups	170-225	8-11	32-47	1-6	490-1225
ramen noodle soups from blocks	160-225	7-9	32-42	1-4	605-1220

Brands of these ramen soups include Nissin, Sanwa, Fantastic Noodle, Oodles of Noodles, and Campbell.

the less fatty . . .

food (one cup serving)	cals	fat (g)	fat (%)	sat (g)	sodium (mg)
chunky chicken noodle	150	5-6	32-35	2	840-850

the leaner . . .

food (one cup serving)	cals	fat (g)	fat (%)	sat (g)	sodium (mg)
chicken noodle or chicken rice	45-150	1-4	8-45	0-1	65-1360
turkey rice	85-100	3	27-34	1	65-820
beef noodle	65-130	2-3	13-40	1	790-1270
beef or chicken barley	65-125	1-3	11-23	0-1	760-930

These soups are very similar in their calorie and fat contents because they contain only small amounts of meat and similar amounts of pasta, rice, or barley.

the leanest . . .

food (one cup serving)	cals	fat (g)	fat (%)	sat (g)	sodium (mg)
low-fat ramen soups in cups	175-185	2	8	0	1030-1280
low-fat ramen soups from blocks	135-170	1-2	6-12	0	450-1500
turkey noodle or chicken & stars	60-70	2	26-30	1	880
wonton	40-55	1	18-23	0	860-1120
vegetable barley	65-95	0-1	0-13	0	290-745

Low-fat ramen noodle soups contain substantially less fat than the regular kind. Campbell and Westbrae brands are examples.

fat-skimming tips:
- eat a plain soup consisting of a meat, such as turkey or beef, and a grain, such as noodles or barley—these usually contain 4 or fewer grams of fat

- look for low-fat ramen soups, which have much less fat than the regular varieties

- remember that ramen soups in blocks contain less fat than ramen soups in cups

see these pages for:
73 vegetable soups
70 meat, seafood, cheese soups
75 bean, pea, lentil soups

cals=calories; fat=grams of fat; %fat=percent of calories from fat; sat=grams of saturated fat; sodium=milligrams of sodium

Soups: Meat, Seafood, Cheese

Since meat, seafood, and cheese contain some fat to begin with, the challenge is to identify those soups that don't add more fat.

things that affect the fat content:
use of cheese: cheese soups are among the fattiest

cream versus broth soups: the cream versions of soups are usually fattier than the broth versions—for instance, New England clam chowder, the kind made with cream or milk, is the fattiest soup listed, while Manhattan clam chowder, the kind made with tomatoes, is one of the leanest

chunky versus regular soups: thicker, denser soups usually contain more fat and calories

this doesn't affect the fat content:
type of meat or seafood: This matters less than what else is added to the soup—clams, lobster, shrimp, oysters, chicken, and beef are all represented in both the fattiest and the less fatty soups below.

the fattiest . . .

food (one-cup serving)	cals	fat (g)	fat (%)	sat (g)	sodium (mg)
chunky New England clam chowder	220	13	52	8	895
nacho cheese	180	12	60	7	800
lobster bisque	190	11	52	7	1080
cream of shrimp	160	10	56	6	860

All of these soups contain cream or cheese.

the less fatty . . .

food (one-cup serving)	cals	fat (g)	fat (%)	sat (g)	sodium (mg)
oyster stew	140	9	58	6	900
cheddar cheese	110-130	6-9	49-62	4-6	740-1095
cream of chicken	90-120	4-8	41-60	2-5	490-1360
sirloin burger	170	7	36	3	920
regular New England clam chowder	80-240	2-8	23-42	1-2	785-1135

the leaner . . .

food (one-cup serving)	cals	fat (g)	fat (%)	sat (g)	sodium (mg)
chili, beef, chunky or regular	140-215	4-5	19-32	2	810-870
chunky chicken	135-145	4-5	25-32	1-2	790-910
fish chowder	105-145	4-5	33-34	2-3	705-960
regular chicken	55-160	2-5	30-39	0-1	565-810
pepper pot	90	4	25	1	970
chunky beef	135-150	3-4	17-23	1-2	775-850

These soups are made with broth instead of cream or cheese.

the leanest . . .

food (one-cup serving)	cals	fat (g)	fat (%)	sat (g)	sodium (mg)
Manhattan clam chowder, reg/chunky	70-130	0-3	0-33	0-2	185-1080
regular beef or beef stew	80-130	1-2	11-23	0-1	480-830
crab	75-95	1	13-16	0	640-1095
broth or bouillon chicken broth	10-40	0-3	0-90	0-1	65-1320
beef broth	10-25	0-1	0-50	0	5-1095
bouillon	5-20	0-1	0-56	0-1	5-1360

Broths and bouillons are low in fat, but can be quite high in sodium.

fat-skimming tips:
  • look for meat or seafood combined with vegetables in broth instead of cream or cheese. Examples are beef stew or Manhattan clam chowder.

  • try refrigerating soup first, so that some of the fat can be removed from the top before cooking

see these pages for:
  67 noodle, rice, barley, ramen soups
  75 bean, pea, lentil soups
  73 vegetable soups

cals=calories; fat=grams of fat; %fat=percent of calories from fat; sat=grams of saturated fat; sodium=milligrams of sodium

Soups: Vegetable
Vegetables are virtually fat-free, so any fat found in these soups is contributed by other ingredients.

things that affect the fat content:
cream versus broth soups: the cream versions of vegetable soups are usually fattier than the broth versions

chunky versus regular soups: thicker, denser soups usually contain more fat and calories

this doesn't affect the fat content:
type of vegetables: most vegetables are so similar nutritionally that this doesn't affect the fat content of the soup

the fattiest . .

food (one-cup serving)	cals	fat (g)	fat (%)	sat (g)	sodium (mg)
chunky corn chowder	255	16	57	10	895
cream of spinach	210	15	64	9	1020
cream of mushroom					
chunky	205	14	64	9	970
regular	110-190	7-11	48-63	4-7	40-1105

All of these soups are cream or chunky varieties.

the less fatty . . .

food (one-cup serving)	cals	fat (g)	fat (%)	sat (g)	sodium (mg)
regular corn chowder	180	9	45	6	1030
vichyssoise	150	9	54	6	940
cream of broccoli	130-140	6-9	42-62	4-6	415-1185

These less fatty soups are also cream soups.

the leaner . . .

food (one-cup serving)	cals	fat (g)	fat (%)	sat (g)	sodium (mg)
cream of celery or onion	95-140	5-7	45-63	3-4	785-970
cream of tomato	95-180	2-7	20-35	1-4	715-880
chunky vegetable chicken or turkey	130-145	5	32-36	2	905-910
cream of asparagus or potato	80-135	3-4	27-45	2	305-1080

the leanest . . .

food (one-cup serving)	cals	fat (g)	fat (%)	sat (g)	sodium (mg)
vegetable, including vegetarian	40-125	0-4	0-50	0-1	65-1120
golden mushroom	70	3	39	1	870
vegetable beef, chicken, or turkey	55-155	1-3	6-39	0-1	85-910
minestrone or gumbo	60-170	0-3	4-36	0-1	65-1095
lower-fat cream of mushroom	70	2	20-30	0	460-950

food (one-cup serving)	cals	fat (g)	fat (%)	sat (g)	sodium (mg)
tomato or gazpacho	55-150	0-1	0-40	0-1	35-945
mushroom, onion, french onion, or borscht	25-80	0-1	0-45	0-1	185-960
vegetable broth	40	0	0	0	80-595

The different **vegetable soups** made with broth are all similar in fat content. Brands of **lower-fat cream of mushroom** include Campbell's and Weight Watchers.

fat-skimming tips:
- for a lean vegetable soup containing 3 or fewer grams of fat per cup, look for a vegetable soup made with broth instead of cream

- make cream soups with low-fat or skim milk

see these pages for:
70 meat, seafood, cheese soups
67 noodle, rice, barley, ramen soups
75 bean, pea, lentil soups

cals=calories; fat=grams of fat; %fat=percent of calories from fat; sat=grams of saturated fat; sodium=milligrams of sodium

Soups: Bean, Pea, Lentil
Beans, peas, and lentils are low in fat, so most of the fat in these soups comes from other ingredients. A major advantage of these kinds of soups is that beans, peas, and lentils are high-fiber foods.

things that affect the fat content:
addition of meat: ham, bacon, or sausage usually adds fat

chunky versus regular soups: thicker, denser soups usually contain more fat and calories

things that do not affect the fat content:
the type of meat: soups made with ham are not likely to be any fattier or leaner than soups made with bacon

the kind of bean or legume: the beans, peas, and lentils used in these soups are similar in fat and calories

the fattiest . . .

food (one-cup serving)	cals	fat (g)	fat (%)	sat (g)	sodium (mg)
higher-fat pea soups					
Lipton brand Cup-A-Soup	185-200	8	36-39	0	880-1105
Pepperidge Farm brand	270	8	27	—	1040
chunky bean with ham	210	7	28-32	3	800-880

These **pea soups** derive their fat from added vegetable oil, the equivalent of two teaspoons in every cup of soup.

the less fatty . . .

food (one-cup serving)	cals	fat (g)	fat (%)	sat (g)	sodium (mg)
bean, rice, and sausage	185	6	29	2	675
bean with ham and bacon	145-230	5	20-33	2	830-1160

the leaner . . .

food (one-cup serving)	cals	fat (g)	fat (%)	sat (g)	sodium (mg)
bean with ham or bacon	120-235	2-5	16-30	0-1	470-895
pea or lentil with bacon	95-145	4	25-39	2	720-920
pea with ham or with ham and bacon	130-215	1-4	4-23	0-2	490-975
plain pea soup	70-200	1-4	11-19	0-2	20-885
plain bean soup	105-170	1-4	2-23	0	720-1265

the leanest . . .

food (one-cup serving)	cals	fat (g)	fat (%)	sat (g)	sodium (mg)
lentil	75-125	0-3	0-26	0	55-705
cream of pea	150	2	14	0	1120
low-fat or fat-free pea	85-140	0-1	0-5	0	55-685
low-fat or fat-free bean	75-140	0-1	0-6	0	175-520

Hain, Pritikin, and Health Valley are brands of **low-fat** and **fat-free soups.**

fat-skimming tips:
  • for a lean soup containing 4 grams or fewer of fat per cup, look for plain bean, pea, or lentil soups or for some of the lower-fat soups flavored with bacon or ham

  • read the nutrition labels of pea soups, because some have unnecessary fat added to them

see these pages for:
  73 vegetable soups
  67 noodle, rice, barley, ramen soups
  70 meat, seafood, cheese soups

cals=calories; fat=grams of fat; %fat=percent of calories from fat; sat=grams of
saturated fat; sodium=milligrams of sodium.

dairy foods

Yogurt and Cottage Cheese

Yogurt and cottage cheese can be low-fat, low-calorie ways to
enjoy the nutritional benefits of dairy products. If you want
foods rich in calcium, however, remember that cottage cheese
is not a good source, because much of its calcium is lost in the
process of draining the whey from milk. Yogurt, on the other
hand, is a good source of calcium.

things that affect the fat or calorie content:
fat content of the milk used to make yogurt or cottage cheese:
this determines the fat content of yogurt and cottage cheese—
the percent is listed on most labels

  the addition of sweeteners: many yogurts contain a substantial amount of calories in the form of sugar or sugar-sweetened
fruit

  flavoring with peanut butter, chocolate, or granola: yogurts
with these ingredients, intended for those who don't really
like yogurt, add fat

  addition of fruit: the more fruit, the less yogurt in a serving—that usually means more calories but maybe less fat

flavoring with plain, coffee, vanilla, or lemon: these flavors require less sugar, so the resulting yogurts may contain fewer calories

things that do not affect the fat or calorie content:
- style of yogurt: whether it is custard-style, Swiss-style, or French-style matters less than the fat content of the milk and the amount of sweeteners added

- addition of acidophilus or other live bacterial cultures: this has no effect on the fat or calorie content

- lactose reduction: special lactose-reduced yogurt, intended for those who have trouble tolerating large amounts of milk, has the same fat and calorie content as regular yogurt

- addition of sprinkles: colored candy sprinkles or jimmies contain no fat, and the small amounts added to yogurt for children have little effect on the calorie content

NOTE: This section looks at refrigerated yogurts. Frozen yogurts are examined in a separate section.

the fattiest . . .

food (1 cup yogurt, 1/2 cup cottage cheese)	cals	fat (g)	fat (%)	sat (g)	sodium (mg)
yogurt with peanut butter, chocolate, toffee	325-365	9-13	25-32	5-8	145-235

Astro is a brand of **yogurt mixed with peanut butter, chocolate, or toffee.**

the less fatty . . .

food (1 cup yogurt, 1/2 cup cottage cheese)	cals	fat (g)	fat (%)	sat (g)	sodium (mg)
low-fat yogurt mixed with granola	290	7	23	4	180-200
yogurt made from whole milk	255	7	24	4	125-165
yogurt made from 2% milk	240-255	5	19-20	3	125-255
plain yogurt made from 2% milk	160	5	28	3	200
cottage cheese made from whole milk	105-125	5	38-41	3	330-445
cottage cheese, whole, mixed with fruit	135-145	4-5	25-32	2-3	255-445

Since granola is the fattiest kind of cereal available (see the section on ready-to-eat breakfast cereals), yogurt mixed with granola will become fattier. Astro is a brand of **yogurt mixed with granola.** Whitney's is a national brand of **yogurt made from whole milk.** Yoplait is a brand of **yogurt made from 2 percent milk. Whole milk cottage cheese** is prepared from milk containing 4 percent milkfat by weight. A cup of **cottage cheese and fruit** has more calories but slightly less fat than a cup of cottage cheese without fruit.

the leaner . . .

food (1 cup yogurt, 1/2 cup cottage cheese)	cals	fat (g)	fat (%)	sat (g)	sodium (mg)
Kissle brand custard	215-240	4	15-17	2	155
low-fat yogurt made from 1.5% milk	225-240	3-4	11-16	2	120-160
plain low-fat yogurt made from 1.5% milk	140	4	26	2	125
low-fat yogurt made from 1.0% milk	220-260	2-3	7-10	1-2	100-160
low-fat, non-dairy yogurt	215	2	8	0	65
low-fat cottage cheese made from 2% milk	95-100	2	18-19	1	330-495
low-fat cottage cheese, 2%, with fruit	105-125	1-2	10-16	1	175-320

Brands of **low-fat yogurts** include Dannon, La Yogurt, and Light 'n Lively. **Low-fat, non-dairy yogurt** is made from soybeans and rice; White Wave is one brand.

the leanest . . .

food (1 cup yogurt, 1/2 cup cottage cheese)	cals	fat (g)	fat (%)	sat (g)	sodium (mg)
low-fat cottage cheese made from 1% milk	80-90	1	10-13	1	30-490
low-fat cottage cheese, 1%, with fruit	95	1	9	1	310-420

food (1 cup yogurt, 1/2 cup cottage cheese)	cals	fat (g)	fat (%)	sat (g)	sodium (mg)
fat-free cottage cheese made from skim milk	70-90	0	0	0	390-550
fat-free sugar-sweetened yogurt	180-215	0	0	0	135-145
fat-free, low-calorie yogurt	90-100	0	0	0	105-180

There are two basic kinds of **fat-free yogurts** made from skim milk. One is sweetened with sugar or fruit and contains nearly as many calories as fattier yogurts. The other kind of fat-free yogurt is sweetened with aspartame and contains only 90 to 100 calories per cup. If you want a fat-free *and* low-calorie yogurt, make sure you select one that contains about 100 calories per cup.

fat-skimming tips:

- look for yogurt and cottage cheese made from the leanest milk

- skip yogurt with peanut butter, chocolate, toffee, or granola

- plain yogurts contain substantially fewer calories than yogurts sweetened with sugar or fruit

TIP: Most yogurts contain live bacteria that help those with lactose intolerance digest the carbohydrate in milk. Look for the special industry seal on the containers, which certifies that the products will contain live bacteria cultures through the expiration date on the label. (Yogurts without the seal may also contain these cultures.)

see this page for:
  169 frozen yogurt

cals=calories; fat=grams of fat; %fat=percent of calories from fat; sat=grams of saturated fat; sodium=milligrams of sodium

Hard, Natural Cheeses

The natural cheese industry has changed dramatically during the past decade. There are now many hard cheeses available that are lower in fat because they're made with partly skimmed milk.

this affects the fat content:

the proportions of whole milk, low-fat, and skim milk used in making the cheese: this determines the fat content of the cheese

things that do not affect the fat content:

sharp or mild flavor: this doesn't affect the fat or calorie content

  cow's, sheep's, or goat's milk: these are close enough in composition that it doesn't make a significant difference in the cheese

the fattiest . . .

food (30 grams)	cals	fat (g)	fat (%)	sat (g)	sodium (mg)
Havarti	120-130	11-12	76-83	8	140-150
brick, Cheddar, Colby, Monterey Jack	120	10	74	5	160-215
blue cheese	105	10	81	5	420-425
goat cheese, hard	130	10	69	6	105

food (30 grams)	cals	fat (g)	fat (%)	sat (g)	sodium (mg)
Stilton	105-115	9-10	70-86	6	
imitation Cheddar or Colby	105-120	9-10	72-74	5	195-205
Muenster	95-110	9	73-80	5	190-270
Roquefort	105-110	9	74-77	6	545-550
Emmentaler	115	9	70	6	
Fontina	110	9	74	6	
queso blanco	100	9	81	6	
Swiss	120	8-9	65-66	5	40-80
Gouda	100-110	8-9	65-81	5-6	200-230
Gorgonzola	100-105	8-9	69-81	5-6	
provolone, Romano	95-115	8	63-70	5	265-360
Limburger	90-95	8	76-80	5	250
gruyère	115	8	63	5	100
Edam	90-100	7-8	63-80	4-5	290-295
gjetost	130	8	55	5	180-250
feta	75-100	6-8	54-96	4-5	190-320
Parmesan	100-110	7	57-63	4	290-450
Tilsit	95	7	66	4	225

the leanest . . .

food (30 grams)	cals	fat (g)	fat (%)	sat (g)	sodium (mg)
mozzarella, whole-milk	95	8	70	4	205-260
reduced-fat cheeses					
Swiss	95	5-6	21-60	3	40-75
Colby	85	4-6	45-68	2-3	5-235

food (30 grams)	cals	fat (g)	fat (%)	sat (g)	sodium (mg)
Monterey Jack	75-95	4-6	51-68	3	80-235
mozzarella, part-skim	85	5	56	3	160-215
Cheddar	75-95	4-5	45-64	3	75-310
provolone	75-85	4-5	51-56	3	150-220
Muenster	75	4	51	3	205
mozzarella	65	3	45	2	260

These **reduced-fat cheeses** are made with partly skimmed milk. There are dozens of brands, including Kraft, Sargento, Frigo, Weight Watchers, and Churny.

fat-skimming tips:
   • try reduced-fat versions of cheese made with part-skim milk

   • mozzarella is a naturally lower-fat cheese

see these pages for:
   85 process cheeses
   187 cheese spreads

cals=calories; fat=grams of fat; %fat=percent of calories from fat; sat=grams of saturated fat; sodium=milligrams of sodium

Process Cheeses

there are three variations on the basic process cheese:
process cheese: this is Cheddar or other real cheese mixed with a small amount of additives to give it a smooth consistency. It has about the same amount of fat and calories as regular hard cheese and usually is sold in slices

process cheese food: this is process cheese with more water and more milk ingredients and less real cheese than process cheese. Most of the cheese slices sold in supermarkets and used in fast-food restaurants are process cheese *food*.

process cheese spread: this is process cheese with even more water and milk ingredients and even less cheese than process cheese food. It can be spread at room temperature.

process cheese food product: this is made with even more water and less cheese, and includes the new low-calorie and low-fat, even non-fat, process cheeses now available

this affects the fat content:
the kind of process cheese: process cheese contains more fat and calories than cheese food, which contains more than cheese spread, which contains more than cheese product

things that do not affect the fat content:
variety of cheese: with the exception of Swiss (which is a slightly lower-fat cheese), whether the cheese is American, Cheddar, Monterey Jack, or another kind doesn't affect the fat or calorie content

sharp versus mild flavor: this doesn't affect the fat or calories

the fattiest . . .

food (1 oz.)	cals	fat (g)	fat (%)	sat (g)	chol (mg)	sodium (mg)
American process cheese	105-120	9-10	72-81	6	25-30	365-555
cheese alternative, higher-fat	95-120	8-10	70-74	1-2	0-5	150-480
Swiss process cheese	95-105	8-9	61-75	5-6	25	365-450

Process cheese, especially American flavor, has as much fat and calories as hard, natural cheeses. **Cheese alternatives** are imitation cheeses made with milk ingredients and vegetable oil. Some, such as Dorman's and Golden Image brands, contain as much fat as conventional cheese. **Swiss process cheese** may contain slightly less fat than American process cheese because Swiss cheese contains slightly less fat than Cheddar.

the less fatty . . .

food (1 oz.)	cals	fat (g)	fat (%)	sat (g)	chol (mg)	sodium (mg)
cheese food	95-100	7-8	64-72	4-5	20-25	360-525
cheese spread	85-95	6-8	60-79	4-5	15-20	130-600

Cheese food is the basis for most of the slices or "singles" you'll find. Brands include Kraft Singles and Land O' Lakes Singles. Some **cheese spreads,** such as Velveeta, can be sliced, while others, such as Cheez Whiz, can be spread.

the leaner . . .

food (1 oz.)	cals	fat (g)	fat (%)	sat (g)	chol (mg)	sodium (mg)
cheese alternative, medium-fat	55-95	3-6	51-68	0-2	0-5	140-385
cheese food product	50-75	2-5	25-64	1-3	5-15	95-505

A brand of medium-fat cheese alternative is Formagg. Borden's Lite-Line and Weight Watchers are brands of cheese food product.

the leanest . . .

food (1 oz.)	cals	fat (g)	fat (%)	sat (g)	chol (mg)	sodium (mg)
fat-free cheese	45-50	0	0	0	0-5	310-460

Fat-free cheeses, such as Kraft Free Singles, are cheese food products with all the dairy fat left out.

fat-skimming tip:
• process cheese contains as much fat as regular cheese—
cheese food, cheese spread, and cheese product have less
fat than regular cheese

see these pages for:
187 cheese spreads
83 hard cheeses

cals=calories; fat=grams of fat; %fat=percent of calories from fat; sat=grams of saturated fat; sodium=milligrams of sodium

restaurant lunches

Hamburgers and Cheeseburgers
Hamburgers and cheeseburgers are the single category of food contributing the most fat in the American diet. It's no wonder when you look at what's in them.

things that affect the fat content:
"deluxe" or "super" burgers: this usually means a high-fat sauce has been added—at Burger King that translates into 8 grams more fat than a "non-deluxe" burger

double versus single beef patties: this nearly doubles the fat

addition of cheese: this adds 3 to 4 grams of fat

addition of bacon: bacon on a burger adds about 4 more grams of fat

this doesn't affect the fat content:
condiments: the lettuce, tomato, mustard, catsup, and onions add few calories and no fat to the burger

the fattiest . . .

food (one)	cals	fat (g)	fat (%)	sat (g)	chol (mg)	sodium (mg)
"ultimate" burgers	705-1030	45-69	54-66	11-32	105-175	935-1810

Restaurants call these "deluxe," "super," even "ultimate" hamburgers. These frequently consist of double beef patties, perhaps bacon and cheese, and almost always a very fatty sauce. Examples are Burger King's Double Whopper and Wendy's Double Big Classic.

the less fatty . . .

food (one)	cals	fat (g)	fat (%)	sat (g)	chol (mg)	sodium (mg)
cheeseburgers with bacon	610-730	39-45	48-58	15-20	80-115	1030-1490

the leaner . . .

food (one)	cals	fat (g)	fat (%)	sat (g)	chol (mg)	sodium (mg)
franchise burgers						
Whopper (Burger King)	630	38	54	11	90	880
Jumbo Jack (Jack-in-the-Box)	580	34	52	11	70	730
Big Classic (Wendy's)	570	33	52	6	90	1085
Big Mac (McDonald's)	500	26	47	9	100	890
double burger with cheese	465-590	27-34	50-54	12-18	70-145	840-1070
double burger without cheese	460-520	25-27	47-49	11-12	95-130	710-890
quarter pound burger with cheese	500-510	28-29	49-52	11	70-115	1060-1090
quarter pound burger without cheese	410	20	44	8	85	650

These **franchise burgers,** which are those products most closely identified with individual chains, are similar in fat and calorie content.

the leanest . . .

food (one)	cals	fat (g)	fat (%)	sat (g)	chol (mg)	sodium (mg)
simple cheeseburger	305-410	13-21	38-46	5-9	40-80	660-800
simple hamburger	265-340	9-15	32-40	4-6	20-65	490-590
reduced-fat plain hamburger	320	10	28	4	60	670

McDonald's McLean Deluxe, a **reduced-fat hamburger,**
contains substantially fewer calories than most other hamburgers.

see these pages for:
224 catsup
226 mustard

cals=calories; fat=grams of fat; %fat=percent of calories from fat; sat=grams of
saturated fat; sodium=milligrams of sodium

Hot Dogs and Buns

things that affect the fat content:
size of the frank: the bigger the frankfurter, the more fat and
calories—especially if it's a quarter-pound hot dog

 addition of cheese or chili: these will add fat

this doesn't affect the fat content:
mustard, catsup, sauerkraut, onions, or relish: these condiments are essentially fat-free

the fattiest . . .

food (one)	cals	fat (g)	fat (%)	sat (g)	chol (mg)	sodium (mg)
quarter-pound hot dog and bun	590	38	58	15	60	1360

the less fatty . . .

food (one)	cals	fat (g)	fat (%)	sat (g)	chol (mg)	sodium (mg)
hot dog with cheese	330	21	57	10	35	920
hot dog with chili	320	19	53	6	30	720
plain hot dog on a bun	280-300	16-17	51	6-7	25	700-710

see this page for:
   56 various kinds of hot dogs

cals=calories; fat=grams of fat; %fat=percent of calories from fat; sat=grams of saturated fat; sodium=milligrams of sodium

Chicken Sandwiches

Chicken sandwiches have become a popular alternative to hamburgers. There are now three basic kinds: fried or "deluxe" chicken sandwiches, grilled or roasted chicken sandwiches, and chicken fajitas.

things that affect the fat content:
frying versus grilling: fried chicken gains fat; grilled chicken loses fat

   "deluxe" type of sandwich: this usually means a fatty sauce has been added

   club type of sandwich: this usually contains cheese and some kind of mayonnaise, both of which increase the fat content

this doesn't affect the fat content:
choice of breast or fillet: this matters less than how the chicken is cooked and what else is added to the sandwich

the fattiest . . .

food (one)	cals	fat (g)	fat (%)	sat (g)	chol (mg)	sodium (mg)
fried, deluxe chicken sandwiches	415-685	20-40	42-55	8-10	40-85	760-1825

These are sandwiches consisting of fried fillets or breast of chicken, smothered with cheese and some kind of fatty sauce. Examples are the Colonel's Deluxe Chicken Sandwich from KFC and Jack-in-the-Box's Chicken Supreme Sandwich.

the less fatty . . .

food (one)	cals	fat (g)	fat (%)	sat (g)	chol (mg)	sodium (mg)
grilled, broiled, roasted chicken sandwiches	265-540	8-21	22-46	1-4	40-65	715-1180

Examples of these sandwiches include Wendy's Grilled Chicken Sandwich and McDonald's Grilled Chicken Sandwich.

the leanest . . .

food (one)	cals	fat (g)	fat (%)	sat (g)	chol (mg)	sodium (mg)
chicken fajitas	185-290	8-9	25-39	3	35	310-785

These **chicken fajitas** consist of vegetables and roasted chicken wrapped in a tortilla. Examples are those sold by McDonald's, Arby's, and Jack-in-the-Box.

see this page for:
108 roast chicken

cals=calories; fat=grams of fat; %fat=percent of calories from fat; sat=grams of saturated fat; sodium=milligrams of sodium

Beef Sandwiches

Beef suffers from a tarnished reputation these days. But some beef sandwiches contain less fat than many chicken sandwiches.

things that affect the fat content:
"deluxe" or "super" style of sandwich: this usually means a fatty sauce and perhaps cheese have been added to the sandwich

addition of cheese: this always raises the fat content of sandwiches

use of "Philly"–style beef: this is a fattier type of beef than roast beef

the fattiest . . .

food (one)	cals	fat (g)	fat (%)	sat (g)	chol (mg)	sodium (mg)
"deluxe" or "super" beef sandwiches	450-620	20-34	40-56	8-10	40-90	800-1950
giant roast beef sandwich	530	27	46	10	80	910
Philly beef and cheese sandwich	500	26	47	6	90	1195

Some of these "deluxe" beef sandwiches include cheese, bacon, mayonnaise, cheese sauce, or ranch dressing.

the less fatty . . .

food (one)	cals	fat (g)	fat (%)	sat (g)	chol (mg)	sodium (mg)
roast beef with cheese sandwiches	405-425	15-18	33-38	4-9	70-85	955-1080

Adding cheese to a roast beef sandwich raises the fat content from 3 to 6 grams.

the leanest . . .

food (one)	cals	fat (g)	fat (%)	sat (g)	chol (mg)	sodium (mg)
plain roast beef sandwiches	310-375	11-15	26-38	5-7	40-80	680-1150
lower-fat roast beef deluxe sandwich	295	10	30	4	40	825

Plain roast beef sandwiches are relatively lean compared to most meals sold in fast-food restaurants. Arby's sells a **lower-fat roast beef** sandwich with a reduced-calorie "deluxe" sauce.

cals=calories; fat=grams of fat; %fat=percent of calories from fat; sat=grams of saturated fat; sodium=milligrams of sodium

Fish Fillet Sandwiches
Fish fillet sandwiches are a perfect example of what happens to food in fast-food restaurants. The fish enters lean and low in fat and leaves deep-fried and smothered with tartar sauce and cheese.

things that affect the fat content:
size of the sandwich: this is the most important factor determining the fat content—the biggest fish fillet sandwiches are the fattiest, the smallest are the leanest

addition of tartar sauce and cheese: these are two of the fattiest ingredients that can be added to sandwiches

this doesn't affect the fat content:
source of fish: there is little difference in fat among the fish used for these fillets

the fattiest . . .

food (one)	cals	fat (g)	fat (%)	sat (g)	chol (mg)	sodium (mg)
fish fillet sandwiches	370-560	16-30	38-49	3-6	30-50	630-1220

Fish fillet sandwiches are so uniform in their content that the only important factor influencing the fat content is their size: the fattiest are the biggest sandwiches, the leanest are the smallest.

fat-skimming tips:
• try to avoid the tartar sauce and cheese

• cocktail or seafood sauce is a fat-free alternative to fat-rich tartar sauce

see this page for:
224 seafood sauces

cals=calories; fat=grams of fat; %fat=percent of calories from fat; sat=grams of saturated fat; sodium=milligrams of sodium

French Fries, Baked Potatoes, and Hush Puppies

things that affect the fat content:
cheese or sour cream toppings: these baked potato toppings, especially the cheese, will raise the fat content

"curly" type of fries: these are thinly sliced "frizzy" french fries which contain 25 percent more fat than regular fries because they have a much greater surface area to absorb the cooking fat

this doesn't affect the fat content:
onion rings versus french fries: overall, there isn't much difference in fat content between equal amounts of onion rings and french fries

the fattiest . . .

food (one)	cals	fat (g)	fat (%)	sat (g)	sodium (mg)
deluxe baked potatoes with cheese, margarine, sour cream	400-730	15-43	31-53	2-15	310-1460

These are potatoes smothered in margarine, cheese, and sour cream. The presence of some broccoli or chives doesn't compensate for that. A potato topped with just margarine and sour cream without the cheese qualifies as a less fatty food.

the less fatty . . .

food (one serving)	cals	fat (g)	fat (%)	sat (g)	sodium (mg)
french fries, extra large or jumbo	450-545	22-26	41-48	5	180-270

food (one serving)	cals	fat (g)	fat (%)	sat (g)	sodium (mg)
onion rings, large to extra large	380-520	23-26	45-54	5	450-960
baked potatoes with margarine and sour cream	465-470	19-25	36-49	7-12	180-205
french fries, large	310-420	16-22	42-50	3-5	190-220
"curly" fries	300-360	16-22	48-60	3-5	165-1030
french fries, medium	300-395	14-21	42-48	3-4	135-240
onion rings, small	240-340	12-19	45-50	3-4	135-630

The size of "extra large," "large," "medium," and "small" varies somewhat from restaurant to restaurant.

the leaner . . .

food (one serving)	cals	fat (g)	fat (%)	sat (g)	sodium (mg)
french fries, small	210-280	10-13	43-49		85-145
hush puppies	145-255	7-12	41-43	3	405-965

Hush puppies, which are fried cornbread balls, differ little in fat from similar amounts of french fries.

the leanest . . .

food (one serving)	cals	fat (g)	fat (%)	sat (g)	sodium (mg)
mashed potatoes and gravy	70	2	26	0	340
baked potato with "lite" sour cream	290	1	3	0	50
plain baked potato	240-270	0-2	0-8	0	20-60

Gravy is a relatively lean sauce, so it's not surprising that **mashed potatoes and gravy** is one of the leanest ways of eating potatoes. Wendy's offers a "lite," **fat-reduced sour cream topping** for their baked potatoes. **Plain baked potatoes** contain only the small amount of fat found naturally in them.

see these pages for:
   126 french fries prepared at home
    97 baked potato toppings

cals=calories; fat=grams of fat; %fat=percent of calories from fat; sat=grams of saturated fat; sodium=milligrams of sodium

 # DINNER

---

meats

beef: prime cuts
beef: choice cuts
beef: select or lean cuts
roast chicken and turkey
pork
ground beef, turkey, chicken, and other ground meats
smoked sausages
seafood: fish and shellfish

---

other dishes

chili without beans, stews, and pot pies
plain beans and bean dishes
potatoes
pasta sauces

meats

Beef: Prime Cuts

Prime is the fattiest grade of beef and is available principally in restaurants. Meat that is well–marbled with fat qualifies for this grade. A 3-ounce serving of cooked prime beef will contain, on average, 2 to 4 grams more fat than choice grade beef and 4 to 6 grams more fat than select grade beef.

this affects the fat content:

the cut of beef: meat from the ribs and shoulder usually contains more fat than meat from the loin, which in turn usually contains more fat than meat from the round or behind

the fattiest . . .

food (3 oz. cooked)	cals	fat (g)	fat (%)	sat (g)	chol (mg)	sodium (mg)
prime rib, broiled/roasted	220-260	13-18	54-64	6-8	70	60-65

Prime rib is the fattiest cut of beef available. Although 3 ounces is no more fatty than a single hot dog, most restaurants serve portions much larger than 3 ounces.

the less fatty . . .

food (3 oz. cooked)	cals	fat (g)	fat (%)	sat (g)	chol (mg)	sodium (mg)
tenderloin, roasted/broiled	195-215	11-13	48-54	4-5	65-75	50-60
top loin, broiled	210	12	50	5	65	60

the leaner . . .

food (3 oz. cooked)	cals	fat (g)	fat (%)	sat (g)	chol (mg)	sodium (mg)
round, tip, roasted	180	9	43	3	70	55
round, top, broiled	185	8	37	3	70	50

fat-skimming tip:
   • prime meat contains 2 to 6 more grams of fat per serving than choice or select grade beef

see these pages for:
   104 choice cuts of beef
   107 select cuts of beef

cals=calories; fat=grams of fat; %fat=percent of calories from fat; sat=grams of saturated fat; sodium=milligrams of sodium

Beef: Choice Cuts

Choice is the grade of beef intermediate between the fattier prime and the leaner select grades. A 3-ounce serving of cooked choice grade beef contains an average of 2 to 4 grams *less* fat than prime, and 2 grams *more* fat than select.

this affects the fat content:
the cut of beef: meat from the ribs and shoulder usually contains more fat than meat from the loin, which in turn usually contains more fat than meat from the round or behind

NOTE: The following calorie and fat values for beef apply in most cases to meat from which all visible fat has been removed.

the fattiest . . .

food (3 oz. cooked)	cals	fat (g)	fat (%)	sat (g)	chol (mg)	sodium (mg)
shortribs, braised	250	15	55	7	80	50
rib, large end, roasted	215	13	53	5	70	60
chuck, blade, braised	225	12	50	5	90	60
brisket, point half, braised	210	12	51	4	75	65

the less fatty . . .

food (3 oz. cooked)	cals	fat (g)	fat (%)	sat (g)	chol (mg)	sodium (mg)
rib, whole, roasted/broiled	200-205	12	50-53	4-5	65	60
flank, braised	200	11	49	5	60	60
rib, small end, broiled	190	10	47	4	70	60
rib eye, small end, broiled	190	10	47	4	70	60

the leaner . . . .

food (3 oz. cooked)	cals	fat (g)	fat (%)	sat (g)	chol (mg)	sodium (mg)
porterhouse, broiled	185	9	45	4	70	55
brisket, whole, braised	185	9	42	3	80	60

food (3 oz. cooked)	cals	fat (g)	fat (%)	sat (g)	chol (mg)	sodium (mg)
T-bone, broiled	180	9	44	4	70	55
tenderloin, broiled	180	9	43	3	70	55
flank, broiled	175	9	44	4	55	70
top loin, broiled	175	8	41	3	65	60
chuck, arm, braised	185	7	36	3	85	55
round, bottom, braised/roasted	165-180	7	36-37	3	65-80	45-55
top sirloin, broiled	170	7	35	3	75	55

the leanest . . .

food (3 oz. cooked)	cals	fat (g)	fat (%)	sat (g)	chol (mg)	sodium (mg)
round, full cut, broiled	160	6	35	2	65	55
brisket, flat half, braised	160	5	29	2	80	55
round, tip, roasted	155	5	32	2	70	55
round, eye, roasted	150	5	29	2	60	55
round, top, braised	175	5	25	2	75	40

fat-skimming tips:
- the loin and the round are the leanest cuts of beef

- three ounces of cooked choice beef can contain less fat than some choices of chicken, hamburgers, frankfurters, or sausage

see these pages for:
107 select cuts of beef
103 prime cuts of beef

cals=calories; fat=grams of fat; %fat=percent of calories from fat; sat=grams of saturated fat; sodium=milligrams of sodium

Beef: Select or Lean Cuts

Select is the leanest grade of beef available to consumers. Some supermarkets sell their own version, which they call "lean" or something similar. A 3-ounce serving of select grade beef will contain, on the average, about 2 grams less fat than choice grade beef.

this affects the fat content:

the cut of beef: meat from the ribs and shoulder usually contains more fat than meat from the loin, which in turn usually contains more fat than meat from the round or behind

NOTE: The following calorie and fat values for beef apply in most cases to meat from which all visible fat has been removed.

the fattiest . . .

food (3 oz. cooked)	cals	fat (g)	fat (%)	sat (g)	chol (mg)	sodium (mg)
chuck, blade, braised	200	10	44	4	90	60
rib, large end, roasted	185	10	47	4	70	60

the less fatty . . .

food (3 oz. cooked)	cals	fat (g)	fat (%)	sat (g)	chol (mg)	sodium (mg)
tenderloin, broiled	170	7	40	3	70	55
rib, small end, broiled	170	7	40	3	70	60

the leaner . . .

food (3 oz. cooked)	cals	fat (g)	fat (%)	sat (g)	chol (mg)	sodium (mg)
top loin, broiled	155	6	34	2	65	60
chuck, arm, braised	170	5	29	2	85	55
round, bottom, braised	165	5	30	2	80	45
top sirloin, broiled	155	5	28	2	75	55
round, bottom, roasted	145	5	28	2	65	55
round, tip, roasted	145	5	28	2	70	55

the leanest . . .

food (3 oz. cooked)	cals	fat (g)	fat (%)	sat (g)	chol (mg)	sodium (mg)
round, top, braised	160	3	19	1	75	40
round, eye, roasted	130	3	20	1	60	55

fat–skimming tip:
 • select grade beef is the leanest available

see these pages for:
   103 prime cuts of beef
   104 choice cuts of beef

cals=calories; fat=grams of fat; %fat=percent of calories from fat; sat=grams of saturated fat; sodium=milligrams of sodium

Roast Chicken and Turkey

Americans now eat more chicken and turkey than beef, in part because these can be relatively low in fat. However, chicken and turkey can have just as much fat as beef or pork—so it pays to know which are the leaner and lighter choices.

things that affect the fat content:

removing the skin: up to half the fat in poultry lies just below the skin: removing skin from chicken eliminates about 5 grams of fat, and removing skin from turkey eliminates about 3 to 4 grams of fat

light versus dark meat: dark meat is the active muscle in poultry with extra stores of fat for energy, so dark meat will contain about 3 to 4 more grams of fat per serving than light meat

choice of chicken or turkey parts: the fattiest to the leanest parts are, in order: back or wing, thigh, leg, drumstick, and breast

chicken versus turkey: on average, a serving of chicken will contain 1 to 2 grams more fat than a serving of turkey

the fattiest . . .

food (3 oz. cooked)	cals	fat (g)	fat (%)	sat (g)	chol (mg)	sodium (mg)
chicken back meat, with skin	255	18	63	5	75	75
chicken wing meat, with skin	245	17	60	5	75	70

the less fatty . . .

food (3 oz. cooked)	cals	fat (g)	fat (%)	sat (g)	chol (mg)	sodium (mg)
chicken dark meat, with skin	215	13	56	4	75	75
chicken thigh meat, with skin	210	13	57	4	80	70

food (3 oz. cooked)	cals	fat (g)	fat (%)	sat (g)	chol (mg)	sodium (mg)
turkey back meat, with skin	210	12	53	4	80	65
chicken leg meat, with skin	195	11	52	3	80	75
turkey wing meat, with skin	195	11	49	3	50	65
chicken back meat, without skin	200	11	50	3	75	80
turkey dark meat, with skin	190	10	47	3	75	65

the leaner . . .

food (3 oz. cooked)	cals	fat (g)	fat (%)	sat (g)	chol (mg)	sodium (mg)
chicken light meat, with skin	190	9	44	3	70	65
chicken drumstick, with skin	185	9	46	3	75	75
chicken thigh meat, without skin	180	9	47	3	80	75
chicken dark meat, without skin	175	8	43	2	80	80
turkey leg meat, with skin	175	8	43	3	75	65
chicken breast meat, with skin	170	7	35	2	70	60
turkey light meat, with skin	170	7	38	2	65	55
chicken leg meat, without skin	165	7	40	2	80	80
chicken wing meat, without skin	170	7	37	2	70	80

the leanest . . .

food (3 oz. cooked)	cals	fat (g)	fat (%)	sat (g)	chol (mg)	sodium (mg)
turkey breast meat, with skin	160	6	35	2	65	55
turkey dark meat, without skin	160	6	35	2	75	65
chicken drumstick, without skin	145	5	29	3	80	80
turkey back meat, without skin	145	5	30	2	80	65
chicken light meat, without skin	145	4	24	1	70	65
turkey wing meat, without skin	140	3	19	1	85	65
chicken breast meat, without skin	140	3	19	1	70	60
turkey leg meat, without skin	135	3	21	1	100	70
turkey light meat, without skin	135	3	18	1	60	55
turkey breast meat, without skin	115	1	5	0	70	45

Turkey breast meat with the skin is the leanest selection you can eat with skin, and **turkey breast meat without the skin** is the leanest meat available.

fat-skimming tips:
   • removing the skin has the most impact on the fat content

• avoid backs and wings because these are the fattiest parts of poultry

see this page for:
92 chicken patties, nuggets, and products

cals=calories; fat=grams of fat; %fat=percent of calories from fat; sat=grams of saturated fat; sodium=milligrams of sodium

Pork
Pork is one-quarter to one-third leaner than it was just ten years ago, thanks to advances in animal genetics and in feeding practices. Today, many cuts of pork are similar in their calorie and fat content to beef and chicken.

this affects the fat content:
the cut of pork: meat from the ribs and shoulder usually contains more fat than meat from the loin, which in turn usually contains more fat than meat from the round or behind

NOTE: The following calorie and fat values for pork apply in most cases to meat from which all visible fat has been removed.

the fattiest . . .

food (3 oz. cooked)	cals	fat (g)	fat (%)	sat (g)	chol (mg)	sodium (mg)
ribs, country-style, roasted	210	13	54	5	80	25
blade steak, broiled	200	12	53	4	70	70

the less fatty . . .

food (3 oz. cooked)	cals	fat	fat	sat	chol	sodium

the less fatty . . .

food (3 oz. cooked)	cals	fat (g)	fat (%)	sat (g)	chol (mg)	sodium (mg)
sirloin roast, roasted	185	9	43	3	75	55
rib roast, center, roasted	180	9	43	3	70	55
90% fat-free ham	135	9	60	3	45	1125
rib chop, center, broiled	185	8	40	3	70	55
loin chop, center, broiled	170	7	36	3	70	50
loin chop, top, broiled	175	7	34	2	70	55

the leaner . . .

food (3 oz. cooked)	cals	fat (g)	fat (%)	sat (g)	chol (mg)	sodium (mg)
loin roast, top, roasted	165	6	33	2	65	40
sirloin chop, broiled	165	6	31	2	80	50

the leanest . . .

food (3 oz. cooked)	cals	fat (g)	fat (%)	sat (g)	chol (mg)	sodium (mg)
tenderloin, roasted	140	4	27	1	65	50
95% fat-free ham	100	4	36	2	45	1095
97% fat-free ham	75-95	3	30-36	1	45	730-1185

Ham is one of the leanest meats available. Brands 95 percent fat-free and 97 percent fat-free include Oscar Mayer, Eckrich, Hormel, DAK, and Plumrose.

fat-skimming tips:
- ham is one of the leanest meats now available

- roast pork tenderloin is almost as lean as skinless chicken breast

see these pages for:
   53 sandwich meats
   26 breakfast meats

cals=calories; fat=grams of fat; %fat=percent of calories from fat; sat=grams of saturated fat; sodium=milligrams of sodium

Ground Beef, Turkey, Chicken, and Other Ground Meats

Ground beef is the most popular form of beef because it's versatile, convenient, and less expensive than other forms of beef. But it's also one of the fattiest ways to eat beef. Regular ground beef usually contains about 27 percent fat by weight, far more than roasts or steaks.

things that affect the fat content:
percent fat of ground beef, ground chuck, ground round: obviously, the leaner the ground beef the less fat, but the differences are greater *before* cooking than they are *after* cooking—cooked *extra lean* has only 2 fewer grams of fat per 3-ounce serving than cooked *lean*.

   ground poultry versus ground beef: ground chicken and ground turkey are leaner than all but the most lean ground beef

   cooking method: broiling or baking ground beef produces leaner meat than frying for regular ground beef only—not for lean or extra lean

this doesn't affect the fat content:
cooking to medium or well-done: both degrees of doneness result in about the same fat content

the fattiest . . .

food (3 oz. cooked)	cals	fat (g)	fat (%)	sat (g)	chol (mg)	sodium (mg)
regular-fat ground beef	245-270	16-19	60-66	6-8	75-90	50-80
hamburger patties	240	17	63	7	80	65
ground lamb	240	17	63	7	80	70

The **regular-fat ground beef** here is 27 percent fat by weight. Three ounces cooked contains about the same amount of fat as a 2-ounce hot dog. **Hamburger patties** are the prepackaged, usually frozen products ready for cooking. These typically contain the maximum permissible amount of fat.

the less fatty . . .

food (3 oz. cooked)	cals	fat (g)	fat (%)	sat (g)	chol (mg)	sodium (mg)
lean ground beef	225-250	15-16	57-62	6	65-85	45-75
extra-lean ground beef	215-230	13-14	53-58	5	70-90	40-70

The **lean ground beef** contains about 21 percent fat by weight, the **extra lean** 17 percent. After cooking, the extra-lean ground beef contains about 2 fewer grams of fat than the lean.

the leaner . . .

food (3 oz. cooked)	cals	fat (g)	fat (%)	sat (g)	chol (mg)	sodium (mg)
ground chicken	160-200	9-14	47-64	3-4	90-125	50
ground turkey	130-210	6-12	36-60	2-4	75-110	60-105
ground veal	145	6	40	3	85	70

Uncooked **ground chicken** and **ground turkey** usually contain from 7 percent to 20 percent fat by weight, depending on how much dark meat and fat is included. The fattier ground chicken contains about as much fat as extra-lean ground beef, while leaner ground turkey contains only one-third the fat of regular ground beef. However, ground turkey and ground chicken can contain much more cholesterol than ground beef, because poultry meat processing sometimes permits cholesterol-rich bone marrow into the ground meat.

the leanest . . .

food (3 oz. cooked)	cals	fat (g)	fat (%)	sat (g)	chol (mg)	sodium (mg)
reduced-fat ground beef	105	3	24	1	50	190

Healthy Choice is a brand of **reduced-fat ground beef** that has been extended with oat fiber. The result is substantially leaner than other forms of ground meat.

fat-skimming tips:
  • ground poultry is as lean or leaner than any ground beef

  • the differences in fat content among regular, lean, and extra-lean ground beef *narrow* after cooking

see this page for:
  115 hamburgers

cals=calories; fat=grams of fat; %fat=percent of calories from fat; sat=grams of saturated fat; sodium=milligrams of sodium

Smoked Sausages
It's possible now to find lower-fat smoked sausages with a quarter of the fat of regular sausage.

this affects the fat content:
use of turkey in place of beef or pork: sausages made with
turkey will be substantially leaner than sausages made with
other meats

things that do not affect the fat content:
choice of Polish sausage, kielbasa, bratwurst, or knockwurst:
these all have the same amount of fat

   choice of pork or beef: these are similar enough in calories
and fat not to make much difference

the fattiest . . .

food (3 oz. serving)	cals	fat (g)	fat (%)	sat (g)	chol (mg)	sodium (mg)
full-fat sausages	255-305	22-27	71-85	8-9	50-105	475-1320

These include all the regular bratwurst, cheddarwurst, kielbasa, knockwurst, and Polish sausages.

the less fatty . . .

food (3 oz. serving)	cals	fat (g)	fat (%)	sat (g)	chol (mg)	sodium (mg)
medium-fat "lite" sausages	195-215	17-18	76-77	5-7	60	730

These **medium-fat "lite"** sausages are made with some or all
turkey meat. Brands include Hillshire Farms and Eckrich.

the leaner . . .

food (3 oz. serving)	cals	fat (g)	fat (%)	sat (g)	chol (mg)	sodium (mg)
lower-fat "lite" sausages	120-165	6-12	45-72	2-4	45-105	760-1200

These **lower-fat "lite" sausages** are up to 90 percent fat-free by weight. Brands include Louis Rich, Mr. Turkey, and Thorn Apple Valley. The leanest have only about one-fourth the fat of regular smoked sausage.

fat-skimming tip:
  • look for sausages made from turkey that are at least 90 percent fat-free

see this page for:
  56 frankfurters

cals=calories; fat=grams of fat; %fat=percent of calories from fat; sat=grams of saturated fat; sodium=milligrams of sodium

Seafood: Fish and Shellfish
Many kinds of fish and shellfish are low in fat, but others contain as much fat as chicken or even beef.

this affects the fat content:
presence of skin: removing the skin from oily fish such as mackerel or salmon will cut the fat by about 3 grams per serving

the fattiest . . .

food (3 oz. cooked)	cals	fat (g)	fat (%)	sat (g)	chol (mg)	sodium (mg)
mackerel, with skin	225	15	61	4	65	70
mackerel, without skin	190	12	47	3	60	95

the less fatty . . .

food (3 oz. cooked)	cals	fat (g)	fat (%)	sat (g)	chol (mg)	sodium (mg)
pompano, Florida	180	10	52	4	55	65
salmon, sockeye	185	9	46	2	75	55

the leaner . . .

food (3 oz. cooked)	cals	fat (g)	fat (%)	sat (g)	chol (mg)	sodium (mg)
salmon, Atlantic and coho	150	7	42	1	50	50
orange roughy	130	7	48	0	20	70
squid	150	6	38	2	220	260
carp	140	6	40	1	70	55
mackerel, Spanish	135	5	36	2	60	55
tuna	155	5	31	1	40	45
catfish, skinless	120	5	38	1	60	65
blue mussels	145	4	23	1	50	315
swordfish	130	4	30	1	45	100
trout, rainbow, skinless	130	4	28	1	60	30
mullet	125	4	29	1	55	60
oysters	120	4	30	1	90	190
sturgeon	115	4	34	1	60	55

the leanest . . .

food (3 oz. cooked)	cals	fat (g)	fat (%)	sat (g)	chol (mg)	sodium (mg)
smelt	105	3	22	0	75	65
clams	130	2	14	0	60	95

food (3 oz. cooked)	cals	fat (g)	fat (%)	sat (g)	chol (mg)	sodium (mg)
halibut	120	2	15	0	30	60
shrimp	110	2	16	0	160	155
sea bass, ocean perch, or rockfish	100-105	2	18-19	0-1	40-50	65-80
scallops	150	1	6	0	60	275
grouper and snapper	100-110	1	10-12	0	40	45-50
pollock and whiting	100	1	9	0	70-80	75-90
sole and flounder	100	1	9	0	50-60	85-90
lobster	100	1	9	0	100	310
crayfish	95	1	11	0	150	60
cod and haddock	90	1	10	0	50-60	60-70
pike, northern	95	1	7	0	45	40
blue crab	90	1	10	0	80	310
Alaska king crab	80	1	14	0	45	910

NOTE: Squid, shrimp, lobster, and crayfish contain relatively high levels of cholesterol.

fat-skimming tips:
* remove the skin from oily fish

* bake or broil with minimal amounts of added oils or fat

see this page for:
60 canned fish

cals=calories; fat=grams of fat; %fat=percent of calories from fat; sat=grams of saturated fat; sodium=milligrams of sodium

other dishes

Chili without Beans, Stews, and Pot Pies

These hearty, hot meals may affect your heart more than you realize. Chili without beans and pot pies are some of the fattiest dishes in the supermarket.

things that affect the fat content:
amount of meat and crust: these are the fatty ingredients, so the more of them, the fattier the dish

   type of meat in *stew*: meatballs are fattier than beef, which is fattier than chicken

this doesn't affect the fat content:
type of meat in *pot pies*: beef, chicken, turkey, and even tuna pies contain about the same amount of fat

the fattiest . . .

food (one-cup serving)	cals	fat (g)	fat (%)	sat (g)	sodium (mg)
higher-fat chili without beans	385-530	29-43	68-73	12-16	855-990
higher-fat meat pot pies	480-685	29-39	44-65	12-15	850-1280

Hormel, Libby's, and Chef Boyardee are brands of **higher-fat chili without beans,** which is one of the fattiest dishes to eat. **Higher-fat meat pot pies** include Mrs. Patterson's and Morton brands.

the less fatty . . .

food (one-cup serving)	cals	fat (g)	fat (%)	sat (g)	sodium (mg)
medium-fat meat or tuna pot pies	395-450	18-25	41-52	7-10	565-1290
meatball stew	240-330	16-23	60-63	7	980-1470
medium-fat chili without beans	315-350	18-21	53-54	9	900-905
chicken stew	275	19	62	4	905
lower-fat meat pot pies	305-360	16-18	40-50	6-7	695-1940

Banquet and Swanson are brands of **medium-fat meat** or **tuna pot pies.** Old El Paso is a brand of **medium-fat chili without beans. Lower-fat meat pot pies** include those from Swanson's Hungry Man and Tyson.

the leaner . . .

food (one-cup serving)	cals	fat (g)	fat (%)	sat (g)	sodium (mg)
higher-fat beef stews	190-250	10-16	41-59	1-5	820-1215

Higher-fat beef stews, which contain less fat than most chili without beans or pot pies, include Dinty Moore, Libby's, and Hormel brands.

the leanest . . .

food (one-cup serving)	cals	fat (g)	fat (%)	sat (g)	sodium (mg)
vegetable and vegetarian stews	155-185	6-8	35-41	0-2	640-850

food (one-cup serving)	cals	fat (g)	fat (%)	sat (g)	sodium (mg)
lower-fat beef or chicken stews	135-180	1-6	6-30	0-1	425-1080

Dinty Moore makes a **vegetable stew,** Worthington Foods a **vegetarian stew. Lower-fat beef or chicken stews** are available from Lunch Bucket, Healthy Choice, Heinz, and Featherweight.

fat-skimming tips:
- skip the chili without beans or find a medium-fat brand

- choose stews over chili or pot pies

see this page for:
  123 bean dishes

cals=calories; fat=grams of fat; %fat=percent of calories from fat; sat=grams of saturated fat; sodium=milligrams of sodium

Plain Beans and Bean Dishes
Beans are enjoying a new popularity because they contain two important nutrients: complex carbohydrates and fiber, especially soluble dietary fiber. Many bean dishes contain 10 or more grams of fiber—much more than the 1 to 3 grams in most fruits or vegetables. And many bean dishes, such as refried beans or pork and beans, are a lot leaner than they sound.

this affects the fat content:
the amount of meat: the higher-fat bean dishes are those with the most meat in them

this doesn't affect the fat content:
choice of vegetarian bean dishes: these may or may not have
less fat than regular bean dishes—it depends on the brand and
the dish

the fattiest . . .

food (one-cup serving)	cals	fat (g)	fat (%)	sat (g)	sodium (mg)
higher-fat chili with beans	285-495	15-28	45-54	5-10	820-1285

Fatty meat makes these **higher-fat chilis with beans** a very
high-fat food. Brands include Heinz, Gebhardt, Hormel, and
Chef Boyardee.

the less fatty . . .

food (one-cup serving)	cals	fat (g)	fat (%)	sat (g)	sodium (mg)
beans with franks	340-365	15-17	41-42	6	960-1105
medium-fat chili with beans	215-290	7-14	25-44	2-6	685-1330

Since frankfurters are a fatty meat, dishes that contain them,
such as beans with franks, will also be fatty. Libby's, Old El
Paso, and Championship are brands of **medium-fat chili
with beans.**

the leaner . . .

food (one-cup serving)	cals	fat (g)	fat (%)	sat (g)	sodium (mg)
beans with pork	220-280	3-6	9-25	1-2	730-1115

food (one-cup serving)	cals	fat (g)	fat (%)	sat (g)	sodium (mg)
plain cooked chickpeas (garbanzos)	270	4	14	0	10
baked beans	220-300	2-4	7-17	0-1	730-1140
refried beans	140-230	2-4	8-25	1-2	540-1120
pork and beans	180-300	1-4	4-14	1-2	730-1000
vegetarian beans	140-280	0-4	0-18	0-1	560-1010

Beans with pork contain slightly more fat than **pork and beans.** And some pork and beans, such as Van Camps, Joan of Arc, and Hunt's brands, contain only 1 or 2 grams of fat per serving. Chickpeas, or garbanzos, have more fat than other beans. **Refried beans** are prepared with only small amounts of vegetable or animal fat. Vegetarian refried beans often contain as much fat as regular refried beans.

the leanest . . .

food (one-cup serving)	cals	fat (g)	fat (%)	sat (g)	sodium (mg)
most plain cooked beans	185-260	1	3-4	0	5-10
fat-free vegetarian chili	225	0	0	0	465

These **plain cooked beans** include white, black, pinto, and kidney beans. Health Valley sells a **fat-free vegetarian chili.**

fat-skimming tips:

• look for leaner brands of chili with beans, as chili with beans can be a very fatty dish

• select bean dishes such as refried beans and pork and beans, which are leaner than they sound

see this page for:
    75 bean soups

cals=calories; fat=grams of fat; %fat=percent of calories from fat; sat=grams of
saturated fat; sodium=milligrams of sodium

Potatoes
Potatoes are a wonderful food, rich in complex carbohydrates
and naturally low in fat.

things that affect the fat content:
addition of cheese, cream, or butter: many potato dishes
involve the addition of these fatty ingredients

    crispy versus regular: "crispy" french fries means fattier
french fries

things that do not affect the fat content:
crinkle cut versus regular fries: these have the same fat content
as regular fries

    choice of instant flakes, granules, or buds: all of these are
non-fat forms of mashed potatoes

NOTE: The calorie and fat contents of the frozen french fries
listed below are *prior* to cooking. Any oil used during their
preparation will increase both the calories and fat.

the fattiest . . .

food (one serving, or half-cup)	cals	fat (g)	fat (%)	sat (g)	sodium (mg)
french fries for microwaving	240-350	11-15	39-52	4	15-465

food (one serving, or half-cup)	cals	fat (g)	fat (%)	sat (g)	sodium (mg)
crispy french fries (uncooked)	150-230	8-15	45-59	2	370-535
higher-fat cheese and creamed potatoes	190-235	9-14	43-55	—	405-540

French fries for microwaving have all their fat already included. Brands include MicroMagic and Act II. **Crispy french fries,** such as Ore-Ida brand, are crispy because of extra fat. **Cheese and creamed potato dishes** include potatoes au gratin, scalloped potatoes, and twice-baked potatoes. Budget Gourmet, Del Monte, Betty Crocker, and Ore-Ida are examples of higher-fat brands.

the less fatty . . .

food (one serving, or half-cup)	cals	fat (g)	fat (%)	sat (g)	sodium (mg)
typical fast-food fries	225	12	47	4-5	150
large baked potato with 1T butter	320	11	31	6	135

Fast-food french fries are discussed in the lunch section. A better choice than butter to put on a baked potato is sour cream.

the leaner . . .

food (one serving, or half-cup)	cals	fat (g)	fat (%)	sat (g)	sodium (mg)
medium-fat cheese and cream potatoes	115-180	4-9	26-49	—	370-660

food (one serving, or half-cup)	cals	fat (g)	fat (%)	sat (g)	sodium (mg)
potato puffs or tots (uncooked)	150-160	7-8	39-45	1-2	280-720
regular french fries (uncooked)	110-160	2-8	11-45	0-1	15-420
mashed potatoes with milk and fat	120-140	5-7	38-45	1-4	85-380
large baked potato with 2T sour cream	285	6	19	3-4	25

Brands of **medium-fat cheese and cream potato dishes**
include French's, Kraft, and Green Giant. **Potato puffs** or
tots fall in the upper range of fat content for frozen french
fries. Some **regular french fries,** such as McCain crinkle cut
brand, contain only 2 grams of fat prior to cooking. The fat in
these **mashed potatoes** comes entirely from added butter or
margarine. Baked potatoes with sour cream is one of the lightest potato dishes.

the leanest . . .

food (one serving, or half-cup)	cals	fat (g)	fat (%)	sat (g)	sodium (mg)
mashed potatoes with milk only	70-80	0-1	0-13	0	55-315
large baked potato, plain	220	0	0	0	15
medium sweet potato, plain	120	0	0	0	10
canned sweet potatoes with syrup	105	0	0	0	40
canned white potatoes	45	0	0	0	355

Leaving out the butter or margarine from mashed potatoes

cuts 4 to 6 grams from the average serving. Plain white potatoes and sweet potatoes are fat-free.

fat-skimming tips:
- look for the frozen french fries with the least amount of fat added—some contain as little as 2 grams per serving

- avoid crispy french fries

- a baked potato with sour cream contains less fat than most other potato dishes

see these pages for:
203 butter or margarine
215 sour cream

cals=calories; fat=grams of fat; %fat=percent of calories from fat; sat=grams of saturated fat; sodium=milligrams of sodium

Pasta Sauces
The popularity of pasta is reflected in all the pasta sauces now available. Many are moderate in their fat, but some are not.

things that affect the fat content:
cream or cheese versus tomato base: higher-fat sauces are based on cream or cheese, the lower-fat ones on tomatoes

addition of sausage: pasta sauce with sausage contains more fat

this doesn't affect the fat content:
flavoring with meat: the addition of small amounts of meat to flavor pasta sauce does not raise the fat level very much

the fattiest . . .

food (half-cup serving)	cals	fat (g)	fat (%)	sat (g)	chol (mg)	sodium (mg)
alfredo	340-540	30-52	79-87	15-26	95-180	820-1080

Alfredo is the fattiest pasta sauce available. Commercial brands include Contadina and Progresso.

the less fatty . . .

food (half-cup serving)	cals	fat (g)	fat (%)	sat (g)	chol (mg)	sodium (mg)
creamy Romano	220	19	78	—	65	490
creamy primavera	190	17	81	—	55	410

the leaner . . .

food (half-cup serving)	cals	fat (g)	fat (%)	sat (g)	chol (mg)	sodium (mg)
white clam sauce	110-130	8-9	60-65	1	10-20	280-460
pasta sauce with sausage	115-170	6-9	48	2-3	15	480-520
Bolognese	140-150	8	48-51	3	20-30	485-520

the leanest . . .

food (half-cup serving)	cals	fat (g)	fat (%)	sat (g)	chol (mg)	sodium (mg)
medium-fat conventional pasta sauces	60-150	3-6	27-56	0	0-5	25-740
marinara	60-90	3-5	45-55	1	0-5	350-740
red clam sauce	70	3	39	0		560

food (half-cup serving)	cals	fat (g)	fat (%)	sat (g)	chol (mg)	sodium (mg)
low-fat and fat-free pasta sauces	50-75	0-2	0-36	0	0	30-825

Medium-fat conventional pasta sauces include Prego, Progresso, Classico, and Ragu. **Low-fat and fat-free pasta sauces** are available from Newman's Own, Hunt's, Weight Watchers, and Pritikin.

fat-skimming tips:
- ease up on the creamy sauces such as alfredo

- choose red sauces like marinara and red clam sauce

- look for the new lower-fat or even fat-free pasta sauces

cals=calories; fat=grams of fat; %fat=percent of calories from fat; sat=grams of saturated fat; sodium=milligrams of sodium

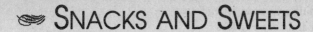 SNACKS AND SWEETS

chips and other crunchy snacks
potato, corn, and tortilla chips
other crunchy snacks
popcorn
nuts and seeds
crackers
snack mixes
rice cakes, crispbreads, breadsticks

candy and other sweets
candy bars
small, loose candies
dried fruit and other snacks made with fruit
granola bars, fruit bars, and other snack bars

frozen desserts
ice cream
ice cream alternatives
ice cream bars
frozen fruit bars

cookies, cakes, pies
cookies
cakes
pies

dairy and meat snacks
spreadable cheeses
dips and salsa

puddings, custards, and gelatins
meat and cheese snacks

---

fruit
fresh fruit
canned and frozen fruit

chips and other crunchy snacks

Potato, Corn, and Tortilla Chips

Chips—potato, corn, and tortilla—are the quintessentially American snack. After all, potatoes and corn evolved in the New World, and chips were first fried here. Although frying in lots of oil is still the most popular way of making chips, some leaner alternatives are now available.

this affects the fat content:
thickness of the chips: thicker slices of potatoes absorb less fat from frying, so kettle-style and other thick chips will contain slightly less fat

things that do not affect the fat content:
choice of flavorings: sour cream and onion, barbecue, and other flavors do not significantly increase the fat content of chips because these flavors are usually fabricated from non-fat ingredients

the color of the corn: whether the corn is yellow, white, or blue doesn't change how much fat it absorbs during frying

organic farming: organically grown potatoes and corn absorb as much fat as other potatoes and corn

source of frying oil: all of the oils commonly used to fry chips in are pretty much the same—shopping around for brands using canola or safflower rather than soybean oil will save less than 1 gram of saturated fat per serving

NOTE: The new official serving size for snack chips is 30 grams, slightly greater than the 28 grams in an ounce.

the fattiest . . .

food (30 grams)	cals	fat (g)	fat (%)	sat (g)	sodium (mg)
potato crisps (Pringles brand)	160-180	10-13	54-70	2-3	145-245
potato chips	150-170	9-11	51-60	2-3	0-235
corn chips	150-170	8-11	41-56	1-2	0-330

Potato chips and **corn chips** are one-third vegetable oil and two-thirds potato or corn. The fattiest national brand is Pringle's **potato crisps,** which are formed from a mash of dehydrated potatoes and water, rather than from sliced raw potatoes, the way most potato chips are.

the less fatty . . .

food (30 grams)	cals	fat (g)	fat (%)	sat (g)	sodium (mg)
thick, kettle, or russet potato chips	140-160	6-10	42-56	2-3	100-345
tortilla chips	140-170	7-9	39-62	1-2	0-345
"lite" potato chips	140-160	6-9	42-45	1-2	115-214

Potato chips such as **thick, kettle-style, or russet** usually contain slightly less fat than thinner potato chips. That's because with these chips there's more potato "inside" protected from the oil and less potato "outside" where the frying oil is absorbed. **Tortilla chips** contain less fat than potato or corn chips because they are toasted prior to frying, a step that reduces their frying time and their absorption of oil.

"Lite" potato chips pick up less oil from frying due to manipulations in the temperature of the cooking oil, the moisture content of the potatoes, and the length of frying time. Ruffles and Pringles brands both have a line of "lite" chips.

the leaner . . .

food (30 grams)	cals	fat (g)	fat (%)	sat (g)	sodium (mg)
lower-fat potato or corn snacks	130-150	4-6	30-39	2	280-495
"lite" tortilla chips	130-135	4-5	30-35	1-3	175-310

Lower-fat potato or corn snacks from Weight Watchers are fried in oil for a shorter period of time than conventional chips. Doritos Light is a brand of **"lite" tortilla chips.**

the leanest . . .

food (30 grams)	cals	fat (g)	fat (%)	sat (g)	sodium (mg)
low-fat tortilla chips or snacks	100-120	1-3	8-27	0	0-190
low-fat or fat-free potato chips	100-120	0-1	0-9	0	0-200

Low-fat and fat-free potato chips and **low-fat tortilla chips** are baked or microwaved instead of fried. Brands include Childer's, Friday Harbor, FitFoods, and Louise's. These contain substantially less fat than regular chips.

fat-skimming tips:
* choose tortilla chips over potato chips

* look for kettle-style or other thick potato chips

* look for new lower-fat and even fat-free versions of snack chips

see these pages for:
138 other crunchy snacks
190 dips

cals=calories; fat=grams of fat; %fat=percent of calories from fat; sat=grams of saturated fat; sodium=milligrams of sodium

Other Crunchy Snacks: Balls, Puffs, Twists, Sticks, Rinds, Chips, and Curls

Here are crunchy alternatives to potato, corn, and tortilla chips. Some, unfortunately, have as much or more fat than potato chips, but others offer less fat.

this affects the fat content:
frying versus baking: snacks that are fried in oil, such as cheese balls or pork rinds, will contain more fat than snacks that are baked, such as pretzels and some bagel chips

things that do not affect the fat content:
flavoring with cheese: snacks coated with cheese "flavor" do not usually contain more fat because it isn't real cheese

using vegetables or fruits instead of potatoes or grains: some chips made from vegetables or fruits have as much fat as potato chips—it's not the source of the chips, but how they're cooked that matters

the fattiest . . .

food (30 grams)	cals	fat (g)	fat (%)	sat (g)	sodium (mg)
french-fried onions	185	14	68	5	195

French-fried onions, such as Durkee French brand, consist of partially hydrogenated vegetable oil (that's the main ingredient) mixed with flour, sugar, and tiny bits of onion.

the less fatty . . .

food (30 grams)	cals	fat (g)	fat (%)	sat (g)	sodium (mg)
higher-fat snack sticks	160-170	11-12	56-62	2-3	10-450
cheese balls, curls, puffs, twists	150-180	8-12	45-62	1-3	200-395
potato sticks	160-170	11	56-60	23	180-375
pork rinds and skins	165-170	10-11	52-56	3-4	560-910
higher-fat snack chips	150-180	8-12	47-62	1-8	75-475

food (30 grams)	cals	fat (g)	fat (%)	sat (g)	sodium (mg)
higher-fat bagel and pita chips	150-160	9-10	51-54	1-2	200-345

All of these snacks have about as much fat per serving as potato or corn chips. Flavor Tree brand is an example of **higher-fat snack sticks. Cheese balls, curls, puffs, and twists** are made from corn and fried in oil. **Potato sticks** have as much or more fat than most potato chips because their greater surface area can absorb more frying oil.

Pork rinds or pork skins are plugs of hog skin cooked in fat. If the skin is smoked, the product is called **bacon rinds or skins.** Among the brands of **higher-fat snack chips** are Bugles, Hooplas!, and Pizza Crunchies. **Higher-fat bagel and pita chips** include Burns & Ricker and Shra Lin's brands.

the leaner . . .

food (30 grams)	cals	fat (g)	fat (%)	sat (g)	sodium (mg)
higher-fat fruit or vegetable chips	145-160	7-10	41-58	1-9	0-320
onion-flavored rings and snacks	130-150	5-8	35-45	1	255-430
pretzels, cheese-filled	140-150	5-8	33-45	2	205-375
medium-fat cheese curls	140-150	4-7	26-45	2	95-325
lower-fat bagel or pita chips	125-140	4-6	28-47	1-2	115-295
medium-fat snack chips	85-150	3-6	23-45	1-2	75-620
medium-fat fruit or vegetable chips	120-130	4	30-33	1	10

Higher-fat fruit and vegetable chips are fried in oil and offer little health advantage over potato or corn chips. These include Hain carrot chips, Health Valley "lite" carrot chips, and Terra Chips. Most pretzels are low in fat, with the exception of **cheese-filled pretzels** such as Combos brand. Cheetos Light is a brand of **medium-fat cheese curls. Lower-fat bagel or pita chips** are made by Pepperidge Farm and That's Entertainment! Examples of **medium-fat snack chips** include Weight Watchers Great Snackers, Zings!, Spicer's wheat snacks, Keebler's Pizzarias, and Frito-Lay's Suprimos. Nature's Favorite is a brand of **medium-fat fruit chips.**

the leanest . . .

food (30 grams)	cals	fat (g)	fat (%)	sat (g)	sodium (mg)
pretzels	105-120	0-2	0-16	0	30-1200
fat-free cheese puffs	105	0	0	0	50-80
fat-free fruit chips	100	0	0	0	155

Pretzels contain little if any added fat and are baked rather than fried. However, thin salted pretzel sticks can have very high levels of sodium. Health Valley is a brand of **fat-free cheese puffs,** Weight Watchers a brand of **fat-free fruit chips.**

fat-skimming tips:
- pass up the french-fried onions

- remember that some fruit chips, vegetable chips, bagel chips, and pita chips contain as much fat as potato chips—read nutrition labels to find the lower-fat varieties

- choose pretzels (without a cheese filling) as a reliable low-fat or fat-free snack

see these pages for:
135 potato, corn, and tortilla chips
153 graincakes
142 popcorn

cals=calories; fat=grams of fat; %fat=percent of calories from fat; sat=grams of saturated fat; sodium=milligrams of sodium

Popcorn: Regular, Microwave, and Pre-popped

Plain popcorn is a lean, filling food. The oil and flavorings are what add extra fat and calories, sometimes in quite large amounts.

things that affect the calorie content:
amount of oil used: naturally, the more oil used in cooking popcorn, the more fat will cling to the final product

pre-popped popcorn versus popcorn you popped yourself: pre-popped bags of popcorn usually contain more fat than microwaved or home-popped popcorn, probably because manufacturers add lots of special flavorings to attract customers into buying a product that can be so easily and inexpensively prepared at home or in a snack bar or office

things that do not affect the calorie content:
use of gourmet popcorn: this isn't fattier or leaner than common popcorn

microwave versus conventionally cooked popcorn: microwave popcorn isn't fattier or leaner, either, though it always contains some fat

butter, cheese, or natural flavors: these all add about the same amount of fat because the flavors are fabricated from oil and other ingredients

the fattiest . . .

food (three cups popped)	cals	fat (g)	fat (%)	sat (g)	sodium (mg)
pre-popped: butter, cheese, natural	120-190	8-14	51-84	1-3	40-410
homemade: oil-popped and salted	165	9	51	2	290

Pre-popped popcorn is the fattiest form of popcorn you can buy. A serving contains as much or more fat than a serving of potato chips. Higher-fat brands include Boston's and Grandma Gibbles.

the less fatty . . .

food (three cups popped)	cals	fat (g)	fat (%)	sat (g)	sodium (mg)
microwave: butter, cheese, natural	75-150	5-9	40-72	1-2	0-560

Regular **flavored microwave popcorn** is not a low-fat snack (but "lite" versions are). Brands include Orville Redenbacher, Jolly Time, and Pop Secret.

the leaner . . .

food (three cups popped)	cals	fat (g)	fat (%)	sat (g)	sodium (mg)
pre-popped "lite"	100-135	5-6	30-51	1-2	0-180

Pre-popped "lite" popcorn contains less added fat. Boston's Lite is one such brand.

the leanest . . .

food (three cups popped)	cals	fat (g)	fat (%)	sat (g)	sodium (mg)
"lite" microwave: butter or natural	50-100	1-3	9-39	1-2	0-170
homemade: air-popped	80	1	10	0	0

Smart Pop, Pop Secret Light, and Weight Watchers are brands of **"lite" microwave popcorn** that have half or less than half the fat of regular microwave popcorn. **Air-popping** produces the leanest results. The one gram of fat in 3 cups of air-popped popcorn represents the small amount of fat found naturally in popcorn seeds.

fat-skimming tips:
- pass up the bags of pre-popped corn

- look for microwave popcorn that contains 3 grams or less of fat per serving

- air-pop corn at home and use grated cheese or spices as a flavoring instead of butter

see these pages for:
213 grated cheeses
138 other crunchy snacks

cals=calories; fat=grams of fat; %fat=percent of calories from fat; sat=grams of saturated fat; sodium=milligrams of sodium

Nuts and Seeds

Nuts and seeds are among the fattiest foods available because they are nature's storehouse of energy to sustain the growth of new plants. But there are still some leaner nuts and nut-like snacks to enjoy.

things that affect the fat content:
choice of nuts: although all nuts are high in fat, some of them, like macadamia nuts, are especially high compared to others, like peanuts and cashews

coating of sugar, chocolate, or honey: these coatings reduce slightly the amount of fat per serving of nuts because the coatings, in effect, replace some of the nuts with a less fatty ingredient

things that do not affect the fat content:
dry-roasting versus oil-roasting: dry-roasted nuts have about the same amount of fat and calories as oil-roasted nuts—that's because nuts are so full of fat to begin with that they can't absorb much more from being fried in oil

seeds versus nuts: seeds, such as sunflower or pumpkin, have amounts of fat and calories similar to those of nuts

NOTE: The new official serving size for nuts is 30 grams, or slightly more than the 28 grams in an ounce.

the fattiest . . .

food (30 grams)	cals	fat (g)	fat (%)	sat (g)	sodium (mg)
macadamia nuts	205-225	19-24	85-96	2-3	0-150
pecans	200-210	19-22	88-95	2	0-105

food (30 grams)	cals	fat (g)	fat (%)	sat (g)	sodium (mg)
walnuts	195-205	19-21	84-95	2	0-5
hazelnuts	200	19-20	87-90	1	0
wheat nuts	215	19-20	81-86	3-4	100-200

A serving of **macadamia nuts** contains the same amount of fat as two tablespoons of butter or margarine. **Wheat nuts** are imitation nuts manufactured from partially hydrogenated vegetable oil (that's the major ingredient) and wheat germ. Anacon Foods and Flavor Tree are two brands. They are an alternative for those who are allergic to nuts, but they are not an especially healthy one. A better choice would be corn nuts (see section on "the leanest").

the less fatty . . .

food (30 grams)	cals	fat (g)	fat (%)	sat (g)	sodium (mg)
pignolia (pine nuts)	155-175	15-19	89-97	2-3	0-20
mixed nuts	180-205	16-18	75-85	3	40-160
almonds	160-190	15-17	74-84	1-2	0-215
pistachios	175-185	15-16	70-78	2	0-295

The amount of fat in a serving of **mixed nuts** depends upon the proportion of peanuts in it. More expensive mixes that contain fewer peanuts will contain more fat, since peanuts are one of the leanest nuts. Likewise, less expensive mixes with a greater proportion of peanuts will contain less fat.

the leaner . . .

food (30 grams)	cals	fat (g)	fat (%)	sat (g)	sodium (mg)
dry- or oil-roasted peanuts	170-195	14-16	69-79	2	0-270
sunflower or pumpkin seeds	170-195	13-16	68-79	2-3	0-280
cashews	175-180	13-15	64-76	2-3	5-215
honey-roasted peanuts	160-180	14	69-78	2	0-195

Peanuts contain less fat than most other "nuts" because they are really legumes, and legumes contain less fat than nuts. **Oil-roasted peanuts** have about the same amount of fat as **dry-roasted peanuts** because peanuts do not absorb much fat during roasting. A serving of **honey-roasted peanuts** usually contains slightly less fat than regular, uncoated peanuts. That's because a small amount of fat-free sweetener is, in effect, being substituted for some of the high-fat nuts.

the leanest . . .

food (30 grams)	cals	fat (g)	fat (%)	sat (g)	sodium (mg)
candy-coated peanuts	155-160	8	42-49	2	25-40
roasted soybeans	140	7	47	1	0
corn nuts	130	4	30	0	180
chestnuts	40-75	0-1	8-9	0	0

Candy-coated peanuts, such as M & M's, have less fat than plain peanuts because fat-free sugar replaces some of the fatty peanuts. **Roasted soybeans** are high in fat compared with most foods, but not compared with nuts. **Corn nuts** are large white corn kernels that are roasted and toasted in oil. They are much lower in fat than nuts because corn is naturally much lower in fat. **Chestnuts** are really a vegetable, and most vegetables are nearly fat-free.

fat-skimming tips:
- go easy on the macadamia nuts, pecans, hazelnuts, and walnuts because these are the fattiest nuts

- select mixed nuts with a higher proportion of peanuts

- substitute honey-roasted nuts for regular nuts

- try corn nuts as an alternative

see these pages for:
47 peanut butter
151 snack mixes

cals=calories; fat=grams of fat; %fat=percent of calories from fat; sat=grams of saturated fat; sodium=milligrams of sodium

Crackers
There are hundreds of brands and varieties of crackers available. Most contain between 4 and 9 grams of fat per serving. The trick is to avoid those with more than this amount of fat and to locate those with less.

things that affect the fat content:
choice of fillings: cheese or peanut butter fillings usually increase the fat content

unrefined versus refined grain: crackers made from 100 percent whole grain usually have less calories and fat than crackers made from refined grain

this doesn't affect the fat content:
the source of refined grain: wheat, rye, rice, and other grains
contain similar amounts of fat and calories

the fattiest . . .

food (30 grams)	cals	fat (g)	fat (%)	sat (g)	sodium (mg)
Chicken in a Bisket brand	170	11	56	2	275
Ritz-type, regular or cheese	150-170	9-11	45-56	2	130-310

"Chicken in a Bisket" brand crackers from Nabisco is
advertised as a cracker that provides the taste of real, cooked
chicken. More accurately, it is a crunchy piece of vegetable
shortening with a tiny amount of "dehydrated, cooked chick-
en" added for flavoring. **Ritz-type crackers**, such as
Nabisco's Ritz and Sunshine's Hi-Ho brands, have as much fat
as potato chips.

the less fatty . . .

food (30 grams)	cals	fat (g)	fat (%)	sat (g)	sodium (mg)
most crackers	120-150	4-9	26-51	0-2	0-495
cheese or peanut butter sandwiches	145-150	7-8	42-45	2	170-315
cheese crackers	130-150	4-9	26-51	1-2	140-495
example: Cheez-It	150	9	51	2	290
grain crackers	130-150	4-9	26-51	1-2	65-405
example: Wheat Thins	140	6	39	0	255
butter crackers	125-175	5-8	39-45	1-3	205-385
Ritz, whole wheat	130-150	6	39-45	2	235-280

food (30 grams)	cals	fat (g)	fat (%)	sat (g)	sodium (mg)
whole wheat	130-150	4-6	30-39	1-2	75-430
example: Triscuit	130	4	30	0	160

Most crackers contain between 4 and 9 grams of fat per serving. Those with cheese or peanut butter tend to be at the high end, those made from whole grains at the low end. But since there is wide variation among brands, read the nutrition labels.

the leaner . . .

food (30 grams)	cals	fat (g)	fat (%)	sat (g)	sodium (mg)
graham crackers	130-150	2-4	15-30	0-1	150-195
saltines and oyster crackers	130	2-4	15-30	0-1	205-450
pretzel crackers	130	2-4	15-30	0-1	170-665

Graham crackers are not made from graham flour, which is whole grain, but they are a lower-fat cracker. Mr. Phipps is a brand of **pretzel crackers.**

the leanest . . .

food (30 grams)	cals	fat (g)	fat (%)	sat (g)	sodium (mg)
low-fat cheese crackers	95-130	0-2	0-15	1	170-345
fat-free pretzel crackers	105	0	0	0	655
fat-free saltine crackers	105	0	0	0	245
fat-free wheat crackers	95-105	0	0	0	170-345

Low-fat cheese crackers and **fat-free wheat crackers** are available from Nabisco's Snackwell brand. Health Valley is another brand of fat-free wheat crackers. **Fat-free pretzel crackers** are available from Nabisco's Mr. Phipps, and Nabisco makes fat-free saltine crackers.

fat-skimming tips:
• pass up the "chicken in a bisket" and Ritz-type crackers

• choose whole grain crackers

• try some of the new low-fat and fat-free crackers available

see these pages for:
187 spreadable cheese
153 graincakes, melba toast, and breadsticks

cals=calories; fat=grams of fat; %fat=percent of calories of fat; sat=grams of saturated fat; sodium=milligrams of sodium

Snack Mixes
These are the mixes of pretzels, crackers, cereal, and nuts often served in bowls for munching on at parties.

this affects the fat content:
amount of nuts: the amount of nuts determines the fat content more than anything else

the fattiest . . .

food (30 grams)	cals	fat (g)	fat (%)	sat (g)	sodium (mg)
mixed nuts	180-205	16-18	75-85	3	40-160

Plain mixed nuts are the fattiest choice for a snack mix. Those with a greater proportion of peanuts will contain less fat (see the section on nuts).

the less fatty . . .

food (30 grams)	cals	fat (g)	fat (%)	sat (g)	sodium (mg)
higher-fat snack mixes	170-180	12-14	62-69	4	10-430
Oriental rice snack mix	165	12	67	0	250

Higher-fat snack mixes, such as Flavor Tree brand, contain a greater proportion of nuts or fried snack ingredients.

the leaner . . .

food (30 grams)	cals	fat (g)	fat (%)	sat (g)	sodium (mg)
medium-fat snack mixes	150-185	8-11	42-60	1-3	140-455

Medium-fat snack mixes include Planters, Ritz, and Pepperidge Farm brands.

the leanest . . .

food (30 grams)	cals	fat (g)	fat (%)	sat (g)	sodium (mg)
lower-fat snack mixes	130-145	5-6	32-42	1-3	290-460

Lower-fat snack mixes contain less nuts and fried crackers and more pretzels and other baked ingredients. Examples are Chex Mix, Cheez-Its, Doo Dads, Gardetto's, and Utz brands of snack mix.

fat-skimming tip:
- look for mixes with less nuts and more pretzels and lean crackers

see these pages for:
142 popcorn

138 other crunchy snacks

cals=calories; fat=grams of fat; %fat=percent of calories from fat; sat=grams of
saturated fat; sodium=milligrams of sodium

Rice Cakes, Crispbreads, Breadsticks, Melba Toast, and Matzo

These are grains with little or no fat added, so they make reliable low-fat or fat-free snacks.

this affects the fat content:

flavoring with cheese: cheese-flavored rice or corn cakes usually have slightly more fat than other flavors

the choices . . .

food (15 grams or half-ounce)	cals	fat (g)	fat (%)	sat (g)	sodium (mg)
breadsticks	65-75	0-2	0-30	0-2	0-125
rice, corn, multigrain cakes	55-65	0-2	0-39	0	0-110
melba toast	55-65	0-2	0-30	0	0-105
crispbreads	45-65	0-2	0-32	0	5-150
matzo	50-65	0	0-9	0	5-95

All of these products contain little or no fat, and there are very few differences among brands. Brands of rice, corn, and multigrain cakes include Chico-San, Hain, Quaker, Mother's, and Pritikin. Crispbreads are the grain wafers made by Wasa, Ryvita, Kavli, Finn Crisp, and JJ Flats.

see this page for:
148 crackers

cals=calories; fat=grams of fat; %fat=percent of calories from fat; sat=grams of
saturated fat; sodium=milligrams of sodium

candy and other sweets

Candy Bars
There's a simple way to identify leaner candy bars: the less chocolate and nuts, the less fat.

things that affect the fat content:
presence of chocolate, nuts, or peanut butter: these ingredients increase the fat content

   use of caramel or nougat: candy made with these will have less fat than candy made entirely from chocolate—for example, a Milky Way or Three Musketeers candy bar has less than half the fat, and a peppermint patty less than one-third the fat, of a milk chocolate bar

   a crunchy, cookie, or cracker filling: candy with these types of filling usually contains less fat because the lower-fat cookie or cracker replaces some of the higher-fat chocolate

things that do not affect the fat content:
the kind of chocolate: dark, white, milk, and semi-sweet chocolate all have about the same amount of fat

   carob versus chocolate: carob candy can contain the same amount of fat as chocolate candy

NOTE: All of the following candy bars are listed for 40-gram or 1.4-ounce servings, which is the new standard serving size for the purpose of nutrition labeling. This permits a fair comparison of the products. However, these candy bars may be sold in amounts that are slightly smaller or larger than 40 grams.

the fattiest . . .

food (40 grams)	cals	fat (g)	fat (%)	sat (g)	sodium (mg)
Alpine White chocolate-almond bar	230	15	59	8	30
Golden Almond chocolate bar	220	15	62	7	25
PB Max	230	14	56	5	145
Snickers peanut butter bar	225	14	58		110
Hershey's milk chocolate-almond bar	225	14	55	6	55
Skor toffee bar	220	14	57	7	125
Nestle's milk chocolate-almond bar	215	14	57	6	25
Bar None	210	14	59	8	40

All of these candy bars contain chocolate, and most of them contain nuts.

the less fatty . . .

food (40 grams)	cals	fat (g)	fat (%)	sat (g)	sodium (mg)
Hershey's milk chocolate bar	220	13	53	7	35
Twix bar	220	13	53		90
Nestle's milk chocolate bar	215	13	53	7	25
Cadbury chocolate-almond bar	215	13	54	6	55
Symphony milk chocolate bar	210	13	56	7	35
carob bar	210	13	56	3	0

food (40 grams)	cals	fat (g)	fat (%)	sat (g)	sodium (mg)
Mr. Goodbar	205	13	57	7	15
Planter's peanut bar	200	13	58	1	100
Heath English toffee bar	215	13	54	6	185
Krackel bar	215	12	49	5	75
Chunky chocolate bar	200	12	51	6	20
Reese's peanut butter cups	195	12	58	9	115
Hershey's dark chocolate bar	190	12	57	7	5
Kit Kat bar	205	11	50	7	40
Bounty dark chocolate bar	200	11	51	6	30
Almond Joy bar	200	11	50	7	55
Whatchamacallit bar	200	10	46		90
Nestle's Crunch bar	200	10	47	6	60
Mounds bar	195	10	48	5	65
Baby Ruth bar	195	10	45	4	90

These candy bars all contain chocolate or carob, and many contain nuts. The **Nestle's Crunch bar** is an example of how the presence of a crunchy interior made of rice can lower a bar's fat content—the crunch bar has three fewer grams of fat than a Nestle's milk chocolate bar.

the leaner . . .

food (40 grams)	cals	fat (g)	fat (%)	sat (g)	sodium (mg)
Rolo chocolate-caramel candy	195	9	40	—	80
Payday bar	190	9	43		150

food (40 grams)	cals	fat (g)	fat (%)	sat (g)	sodium (mg)
Snickers bar	180	9	44	5	110
Fifth Avenue bar	185	8	41	—	75
Clark bar	190	7	33		35
Tiger's Milk nutrition bar	185	7	34		115
Butterfinger bar	175	7	38	3	55
Oh Henry! bar	175	7	35	3	95
Milky Way dark chocolate bar	175	6	33	3	90
Milky Way milk-chocolate bar	165	6	33	3	95
Three Musketeers bar	165	5	28	3	80

These candy bars consist of ingredients in addition to chocolate and nuts. Note that the Milky Way and Three Musketeer bars, which contain a substantial amount of nougat, have less than half the fat of milk chocolate bars.

the leanest . . .

food (40 grams)	cals	fat (g)	fat (%)	sat (g)	sodium (mg)
Charlestown Chew	170	4	23	—	55
York peppermint patties	140	4	24	0	15
Tootsie Roll	160	3	17	1	40
Bit-O-Honey	155	3	18		105
Sugar Daddy pop	155	1	6	0	85
licorice	130-150	1	4-10	0	15-200

The chocolate in these candies is limited to a coating on the

peppermint patties and Charlestown Chews. None have nuts.

fat-skimming tip:
* look for candy bars with ingredients other than chocolate or nuts

see these pages for:
158 loose candies
161 fruit snacks

cals=calories; fat=grams of fat; %fat=percent of calories from fat; sat=grams of saturated fat; sodium=milligrams of sodium

Small, Loose Candies

Small, loose candies can have as much fat as candy bars. But, unlike candy bars, there are also many choices that contain little or no fat.

things that affect the fat content:
presence of chocolate, nuts, or peanut butter: Candies containing these ingredients will contain more fat than candies without these ingredients

amount of chocolate: The more chocolate in a candy, the more fat it will contain (a mint coated with chocolate has only one-fifth the fat of a solid chocolate kiss)

this doesn't affect the fat content:
flavors: most flavors are manufactured from extracts or synthetic compounds, neither of which contain much fat.

the fattiest . . .

food (40 grams)	cals	fat (g)	fat (%)	sat (g)	sodium (mg)
Almond Roca	230	14	56	5	45
Hershey's Kisses with Almonds	230	14	56	—	35
chocolate truffles	195	14	63	9	25
Hershey's Kisses	215	13	54	7	35
chocolate-coated peanuts	205-215	13	54-59	5	15
candy-coated peanuts	205-215	10-11	42-49	2	30-50

All of these candies are made with chocolate or nuts, or both. Goobers is a brand of chocolate-coated peanuts, M & M's a brand of candy-coated peanuts.

the less fatty . . .

food (40 grams)	cals	fat (g)	fat (%)	sat (g)	sodium (mg)
Reese's Pieces candy-coated peanut butter	200	9	40	7	60
non-pareils, chocolate	200	7-9	32-39		20
candy-coated chocolate	200	8	42		40
malted milk balls	185	7	35		55
Milk Duds	170	6	32	4	95
chocolate-coated raisins	155-185	6-7	30-38	3-4	10-45
peanut brittle	150-185	4-7	26-35	1	55-195
caramel popcorn	155-185	3-7	17-35	0-1	85-255

These candies contain lesser amounts of chocolate and nuts than the fattiest candies above. Brach's makes chocolate non-pareils. M & M's is a brand of candy-coated chocolate, Raisinets a brand of chocolate-coated raisins, and Cracker Jack a brand of caramel popcorn.

the leaner . . .

food (40 grams)	cals	fat (g)	fat (%)	sat (g)	sodium (mg)
Pearson's Nips	170	3-6	15-30	—	85-115
caramels	150-170	4-5	23-30	3	100-105
butter toffee	170	4	23	3	150
Starburst Fruit Chews	170	4	21	1	20
chocolate-coated mints	115-170	3-4	16-24	1	15
butterscotch hard candy	155-170	0-3	0-15	0-1	0-155
Skittles fruit candy	170	1	7	0	20
taffy	150	1	8	1	35

None of these candies contain nuts and only the Nips and mints contain small amounts of chocolate. Werther's is a brand of butter toffee.

the leanest . . .

food (40 grams)	cals	fat (g)	fat (%)	sat (g)	sodium (mg)
mints, dessert or butter	155-160	0	0	0	0
circus peanuts	155	0	0	0	5
hard candy	150	0	0	0	0-15
candy corns	145	0	0	0	135
gum balls	145	0	0	0	5
jelly beans	145	0	0	0	5-15

food (40 grams)	cals	fat (g)	fat (%)	sat (g)	sodium (mg)
fruit jelly candy	145	0	0	0	5-30
Juijfruits	145	0	0	0	70
Smarties or Snappy Tarts	145	0	0	0	0
lollipops	145	0	0	0	15
Good & Plenty	135	0	0	0	80
marshmallows	120-135	0	0	0	30-65
gummy bears	120	0	0	0	0

All of these candies are fat-free. Their principal ingredient is sugar.

fat-skimming tip:
  • look for candy with ingredients other than chocolate or nuts

see these pages for:
  154 candy bars
  161 dried fruit candy
  164 granola bars

cals=calories; fat=grams of fat; %fat=percent of calories from fat; sat=grams of saturated fat; sodium=milligrams of sodium

Dried Fruit and Other Snacks Made with Fruit

Fruit is naturally low in fat, so it's what's coated on and mixed with the fruit that adds any fat—and calories.

things that affect the fat content:
mixing fruit with nuts: the addition of nuts or coconut will increase the fat content of a fruit mixture

coating: coating dried fruit such as raisins with chocolate, carob, or yogurt will also increase the fat content

this doesn't affect the fat content:
the source of dried fruit: all dried fruits are similar in calorie content

the fattiest . . .

food (30 grams)	cals	fat (g)	fat (%)	sat (g)	sodium (mg)
trail mixes of fruit and nuts	140-145	8-9	48-59	1-2	5-70

Mixtures of dried fruit and nuts called **trail mixes** are convenient as snacks during travel. The proportion of nuts in them determines fat content.

the less fatty . . .

food (30 grams)	cals	fat (g)	fat (%)	sat (g)	sodium (mg)
fruit chips, medium-fat	130	5	38	1	15
tropical trail mix	125	5	38	3	5
raisins, yogurt-coated	130-140	3-5	23-38	0	10-20
raisins, chocolate- or carob-coated	120	4	33	2-3	15

Fruit chips are slices of fruit either fried in fat or dried. Nature's Favorite brand is an example of **medium-fat apple chips. Tropical trail mix** contains less fat than regular trail mix because it has less nuts. **Yogurt-coated raisins** are raisins with a pale-colored vegetable oil and milk protein concoction applied to the outside. **Coating raisins with chocolate** adds about 4 grams of fat to the fruit.

the leaner . . .

food (30 grams)	cals	fat (g)	fat (%)	sat (g)	sodium (mg)
children's fruit snacks	105-125	1-3	5-23	1-2	10-120

Children's fruit snacks are the roll-ups, leathers, sheets, dinosaurs and cartoon characters fabricated from fruit, sugar, and partially hydrogenated vegetable oil. Typical brands are Betty Crocker Fruit Roll-Ups, Farley, and Fruit Corners.

the leanest . . .

food (30 grams)	cals	fat (g)	fat (%)	sat (g)	sodium (mg)
plain, dried fruit	55-120	0	0	0	0-35
fruit chips, fat-free	105	0	0	0	160-170

Plain, dried fruit includes raisins, apricots, dates, prunes, apples, and any other 100 percent dried fruit. Weight Watchers brand is an example of **fat-free fruit chips.**

fat-skimming tip:
  • choose plain raisins and dried fruit for the lowest-fat fruit snack

see this page for:
  197 fresh fruit

cals=calories; fat=grams of fat; %fat=percent of calories from fat; sat=grams of saturated fat; sodium=milligrams of sodium

Granola Bars, Fruit Bars, and Other Snack Bars

Granola bars have an image of being wholesome, particularly nutritious snacks. The truth, however, is that many are not much different than chocolate candy. But this shouldn't be surprising, since granola cereal is the fattiest kind of cereal available.

things that affect the fat content:

chocolate or fudge coating: these raise the fat content, making the coated varieties of granola and other snack bars some of the fattiest

fruit filling: bars with fruit filling have less fat than those made with nuts or peanut butter

this doesn't affect the fat content:

soft and chewy versus hard granola bars: both can be higher-fat or lower-fat

NOTE: All of the following bars are listed for 40-gram or 1.4-ounce servings, which is the new standard serving size for the purpose of nutrition labeling. This permits a fair comparison of the products. However, these snack bars may be sold in amounts that are slightly smaller or larger than 40 grams.

the fattiest . . .

food (40-gram bar)	cals	fat (g)	fat (%)	sat (g)	sodium (mg)
higher-fat granola bars	195-220	11-14	48-59	6-8	60-90
chocolate- or fudge-coated granola bars	185-215	9-13	45-55	7	60-90
diet bars	190-210	10-12	45-54	2	85-255
breakfast bars	195-200	11	47-50		175-190

Higher-fat granola bars, such as some Kudos and Barbara's Bakery bars, contain the most added fat, chocolate, or nuts. Brands of **chocolate- or fudge–coated granola bars** include Quaker, Hershey, Little Debbie, and Sunbelt. Carnation Slender and Figurines **diet bars** are intended as meal or snack replacements, but they contain the same amount of calories and fat as granola bars when eaten in the same amounts. Carnation **breakfast bars** are fortified with some nutrients.

the less fatty . . .

food (40-gram bar)	cals	fat (g)	fat (%)	sat (g)	sodium (mg)
dessert bars	200-220	7-10	33-41	2	110-200
most granola bars	140-200	6-10	28-46	1-7	20-170

Dessert bars are baked from General Mills' mixes. **Most granola bars** contain from 6 to 10 grams of fat per serving, about the same as a Snickers candy bar. These include Nature Valley, Kudos Pan Squares, Quaker Chewy, and Nature's Choice brands.

the leaner . . .

food (40-gram bar)	cals	fat (g)	fat (%)	sat (g)	sodium (mg)
"lite" granola bars	140-170	3-6	18-30	1	5-115
Nutri-Grain brand fruit-grain bars	150	4	26	1	65-70
fruit bars	95-155	2-4	13-28	1-3	15-115

"Lite" granola bars are available from Kellogg's, Barbara's Bakery, and Fi-Bar. These contain from one–quarter to one-half the fat of regular granola bars. **Nutri-Grain fruit and grain bars** are one of the leanest national-brand bars available. Health Valley, Interbake, and Fi-Bar are brands of **fruit bars.**

the leanest . . .

food (40-gram bar)	cals	fat (g)	fat (%)	sat (g)	sodium (mg)
fat-free fruit bars	130	0	0	0	10
fat-free granola bars	130	0	0	0	10

Fat-free fruit bars and **fat-free granola bars** are available from Health Valley.

fat-skimming tips:
- skip the chocolate and fudge coatings and look instead for fruit

- try the lower-fat bars, such as Nutri-Grain fruit and cereal bars, or the low-fat and fat-free granola bars

see these pages for:
154 candy bars
39 instant breakfast bars
164 granola

cals=calories; fat=grams of fat; %fat=percent of calories from fat; sat=grams of saturated fat; sodium=milligrams of sodium

frozen desserts

Ice Cream
Nowhere has the development of new, lower-fat foods had more impact than on frozen desserts. This section describes

"real" ice cream—the mixture of cream, milk, and sugar specified by federal law. Alternatives to ice cream, such as "light" ice cream, ice milk, sorbet, and frozen yogurt, are discussed in another section.

things that affect the fat content:
rich, gourmet versus conventional brands: more expensive gourmet ice creams use more cream and egg yolks than regular ice creams

flavoring with nuts or peanut butter: ice creams with these high-fat ingredients will usually contain greater amounts of fat

flavoring with fruit: fruit-flavored ice cream is frequently the least fatty (strawberry is often the leanest choice).

the fattiest . . .

food (half-cup serving)	cals	fat (g)	fat (%)	sat (g)	chol (mg)	sodium (mg)
gourmet ice creams	230-360	13-24	49-68	5-10	45-95	40-160
Haagen-Dazs brand	250-330	15-21	59-64	8-10	95-145	40-140
Haagen-Dazs Extraas	300-340	18-22	54-61	7-10	75-110	75-130
Frusen Gladje brand	230-300	13-21	51-68	9-10	55-90	60-160
Ben & Jerry's	250-310	16-20	51-61		45-95	55-115
higher-fat flavors Heath bar	280-360	17-24	51-60		55-85	60-115
pecan, walnut, or other nut	270-350	17-24	53-68	5-9	60	55-160
lower-fat flavors strawberry or other fruit	230-280	15-16	51-59	10	65	40-65

Gourmet ice cream can contain twice the fat of ordinary ice cream. The **higher-fat flavors** usually contain nuts, the **lower-fat flavors** fruit, most commonly strawberry.

the less fatty . . .

food (half-cup serving)	cals	fat (g)	fat (%)	sat (g)	chol (mg)	sodium (mg)
regular ice cream	120-190	5-12	28-60	1-6	15-35	30-135
higher-fat flavors nuts or peanut butter	155-190	9-12	51-60	3-5	15-30	40-125
lower-fat flavors strawberry or other fruit	120-140	5-7	35-45	2-5	15-30	40-70

National brands of **regular ice cream** include Borden's, Breyer's, Lucerne, Land O'Lakes, and Sealtest. As with the gourmet kind, the higher-fat flavors usually contain nuts and the lower-fat are fruit flavors, most commonly strawberry.

fat-skimming tips:
   • think twice about gourmet ice cream because there are so many leaner options available

   • choose fruit instead of nut flavors

   • when in doubt, choose strawberry

see these pages for:
   169 ice cream alternatives
   221 toppings

cals=calories; fat=grams of fat; %fat=percent of calories from fat; sat=grams of saturated fat; sodium=milligrams of sodium

Ice Cream Alternatives:
"Lite" Ice Cream, Frozen Yogurt, Sorbet, and Other Similar Desserts

There are now many lower-fat alternatives to ice cream. But you must know what to look for, because nearly every option is available in higher-fat versions, as well as in medium- and lower-fat versions.

things that affect the fat content:
flavoring with nuts or peanut butter: as always, these ingredients raise the fat content

   soft-serve versus hard frozen dessert: since the soft-serve contains more water, it will usually have less fat

this doesn't affect the fat content:
use of non-dairy ingredients: desserts made from soybeans or rice instead of milk ingredients may or may not have less fat than dairy desserts, since it depends upon how much vegetable fat is added during manufacturing (indeed, one soybean-based dessert is the fattiest available alternative to ice cream).

the fattiest . . .

food (half-cup serving)	cals	fat (g)	fat (%)	sat (g)	chol (mg)	sodium (mg)
higher-fat non-dairy dessert	200-240	10-17	45-64	2-3	0	95-130
for comparison: regular ice cream	120-190	5-12	28-60	1-6	15-35	30-135

Regular ice cream is listed here for comparison. Higher-fat non-dairy desserts include Tofutti soybean-based desserts and some flavors of Ice Bean, a frozen dessert made from rice.

These contain as much or more fat than regular ice cream, though they do have less saturated fat and no cholesterol.

the less fatty . . .

food (half-cup serving)	cals	fat (g)	fat (%)	sat (g)	chol (mg)	sodium (mg)
gourmet "lite" ice cream	190-240	7-11	33-41		25-45	
higher-fat frozen yogurt	170-220	7-9	30-43	3-4	5-55	60-100
sorbet and cream	180-200	7-8	35-40	4	60	30-35

Ben & Jerry's "Light" is an example of a **gourmet "lite" ice cream** that contains as much fat as regular ice cream. **Higher-fat frozen yogurts** include Haagen-Dazs Extraas, Dannon's Pure Indulgence, and some Colombo flavors. Haagen-Dazs makes **sorbet and cream.**

the leaner . . .

food (half-cup serving)	cals	fat (g)	fat (%)	sat (g)	chol (mg)	sodium (mg)
medium-fat non-dairy desserts	100-140	2-7	16-45	0-1	0	15-80
medium-fat frozen yogurts	105-200	3-6	15-34	0-2	5-50	40-160
medium-fat "lite" dairy desserts	90-150	3-6	25-45	0-3	10-15	35-120
soft-serve frozen yogurt	115	4	32-34	2-3	0-5	65-70

Medium-fat non-dairy desserts include most rice- and soybean-based frozen desserts. **Medium-fat frozen yogurt** brands include Ben & Jerry's, Frusen Gladje, Elan, Kemp's, TCBY, I Can't Believe It's Yogurt, and Yoplait. **Medium-fat "lite" dairy desserts** are available from Sweet 'n Low,

Baskin-Robbins, Edy's, Dreyer's, Hood, Breyer's, Light 'n Lively, Weight Watchers, and Lucerne. Some of these dairy desserts are the equivalent of ice milk, a name for lower-fat ice cream that is not used as much as it used to be.

the leanest . . .

food (half-cup serving)	cals	fat (g)	fat (%)	sat (g)	chol (mg)	sodium (mg)
soft-serve ice milk	110	2	19	2	5	80
lower-fat frozen yogurt	90-160	1-2	8-20	0-1	5-15	45-75
sherbet	95-135	1-2	7-19	0-1	5	25-40
lower-fat "lite" dairy desserts	80-160	1-2	6-23	0-1	0-5	50-100
sorbet and ices	75-140	0-1	0-10	0	0	5-10
fat-free dairy desserts	90-130	0	0	0	0-5	0-80
fat-free frozen yogurt	70-110	0	0	0		35-55
fat-free non-dairy desserts	90-100	0	0	0	0	60-180

Lower-fat frozen yogurt brands include Edy's Inspiration and Breyer's. **Sherbet** is prepared from a mixture of fruit and a small amount of milkfat. Healthy Choice, Sweet 'n Low, Edy's American Dream, Hood Free, and Weight Watchers are brands of **lower-fat "lite" dairy desserts. Sorbets** and **ices** are mostly fruit and water. **Fat-free dairy desserts** brands are Simple Pleasures, Baskin-Robbins, Sealtest Free, Lucerne Free, and Weight Watchers. **Fat-free frozen yogurt** is made by TCBY, Sealtest, Dannon, and Kemp's. Tofutti Free is a brand of **fat-free non-dairy dessert.**

fat-skimming tips:
- try one of the dozens of lower-fat and even fat-free frozen desserts

- for each kind of frozen dessert, there is usually a range of higher-fat to lower-fat choices, so read the nutrition labels

see these pages for:
166 real ice cream
221 toppings

cals=calories; fat=grams of fat; %fat=percent of calories from fat; sat=grams of saturated fat; sodium=milligrams of sodium

Ice Cream Bars
Balancing the tempting chocolate and nut gourmet ice cream bars are a variety of lower-fat alternatives.

things that affect the fat content:
flavoring with chocolate or nuts: as always, these fattier ingredients raise the fat content

ice cream versus ice milk or frozen yogurt: bars that contain real ice cream will have more fat than those made with ice milk or frozen yogurt

the fattiest . . .

food (one serving)	cals	fat (g)	fat (%)	sat (g)	chol (mg)	sodium (mg)
higher-fat frozen bars						
Haagen-Dazs	210-390	14-27	60-70	6-15	35-100	50-170
Ben & Jerry's	240-350	14-27	48-69	6-13	25-50	65-195
Dove	335-380	21-25	56-59	12-13	35-40	45-100

food (one serving)	cals	fat (g)	fat (%)	sat (g)	chol (mg)	sodium (mg)
higher-fat candy: O Henry! ice cream bar	320	20	56			75

These ice cream bars are the equivalent of a serving of higher-fat gourmet ice cream.

the less fatty . . .

food (one serving)	cals	fat (g)	fat (%)	sat (g)	chol (mg)	sodium (mg)
medium-fat frozen bars and cones						
Elan frozen yogurt bars	230-260	13-16	51-55		10	45
fast-food cones and sundaes	260-350	8-16	26-56	5-9	10-30	50-290
Carnation bars	150-225	9-15	54-61			
Good Humor chocolate chip sandwich	320	15	42	9	20	190
medium-fat candy bar desserts	180-220	11-14	52-60	6-7	15	35-65
Good Humor chocolate-coated bar	160	11	62	9	15	35
Eskimo Pie chocolate-coated bar	140	11	71			30

Medium-fat fast-food cones and sundaes are available at Dairy Queen and Hardee's. **Medium-fat candy bar desserts** include frozen Snickers, Nestle's Crunch, Butterfinger, and Milky Way.

the leaner . . .

food (one serving)	cals	fat (g)	fat (%)	sat (g)	chol (mg)	sodium (mg)
Klondike chocolate-coated bar	230	9	35		10	220
lower-fat chocolate-coated bars	100-170	7-9	48-63		0-5	35-120
ice cream sandwiches	130-190	4-6	26-35	3-4	5-15	110-155
Rondo's small chocolate bars	60-70	4	51-60	2	5-15	10-20
"lite" ice cream sandwiches	90-160	2-4	13-23	0-1	5-10	110-200

Lower-fat chocolate-coated bars are available from Weight Watchers, Gold Bond, and Good Humor. Ultra Slim Fast and Klondike are two brands of **"lite" ice cream sandwiches.**

the leanest . . .

food (one serving)	cals	fat (g)	fat (%)	sat (g)	chol (mg)	sodium (mg)
pudding pops	70-80	1-3	11-34	0-2	0	50-90
lower-fat fast-food sundaes/cones	105-270	0-3	0-11	0-2	0-15	25-180
fudge bars, "lite" and regular	30-125	0-1	0-36	0-1	0-5	30-120
very low-fat ice cream bars	40-100	0-1	0-15	0-1	0-5	5-75
fat-free ice cream sandwich	130	0	0	0	0	150
fat-free fudge swirl bars	80-90	0	0	0	0	30-40

Pudding Pops are made by Jell-O. **Lower-fat fast-food sundaes and cones** are available at McDonald's. **Fudge bars** and **fudgsicles** are reliable low-fat choices. **Very-low fat ice cream bars** are made by Weight Watchers and Crystal Light. Eskimo Pie and Weight Watchers are two brands of **fat-free ice cream sandwiches,** and Sealtest is a brand of **fat-free fudge swirl bars.**

cals=calories; fat=grams of fat; %fat=percent of calories from fat; sat=grams of saturated fat; sodium=milligrams of sodium

Frozen Fruit Bars
These are frozen desserts whose primary ingredient is a fruit or fruit flavor, not milk or cream.

Since fruit is naturally almost fat-free, these products vary mostly in the amount of calories they contain. Almost all are low-fat, low-calorie choices.

this affects the calorie content:
addition of cream: the addition of cream or ice cream raises the fat and calorie content

things that do not affect the calorie content:
fruit juice versus fruit flavor: both have about the same amount of calories

the particular fruit: fruits don't vary enough in calories to matter when it comes to eating a frozen fruit bar

the fattiest . . .

food (one)	cals	fat (g)	fat (%)	sat (g)	sodium (mg)
higher-fat fruit and cream bars	120-175	4-9	30-51	3-6	0-20

Higher-fat fruit and cream bars have more cream and less fruit than other brands. Examples include Dole Fruit & Cream, Haagen-Dazs, and FrozFruit brands.

the less fatty . . .

food (one)	cals	fat (g)	fat (%)	sat (g)	sodium (mg)
medium-fat fruit and ice cream swirl bars	70-80	3	34-39	0	0

Medium-fat fruit and ice cream swirl bars are made by Chiquita and Carnation.

the leaner . . .

food (one)	cals	fat (g)	fat (%)	sat (g)	sodium (mg)
lower-fat fruit and cream bars	30-95	0-2	5-36	0-1	0-40
sherbet push-ups	55-90	1	8-10	0-1	20
fruit and yogurt bars	60-80	1	6-8	0-1	15-20
Italian ice bars	110-140	1	3-4	0	0
fruit-flavored bars	10-90	0-1	0-35	0	0-25
juice bars	10-100	0-1	0-11	0	0-15

food (one)	cals	fat (g)	fat (%)	sat (g)	sodium (mg)
gelatin pops	30-35	0	0	0	20-25
ice pops	10-50	0	0	0	5-10

Lower-fat fruit and cream bars include Chiquita, Good Humor, Sunkist, Fi-Bar, and Yoplait brands. The Flintstone and Good Humor brands of **push-ups** consist of sherbet and fruit flavoring. **Fruit and yogurt bars** are made by Dole. Good Humor makes **Italian ice bars. Fruit-flavored bars** are available from Crystal Light, Dole SunTops, Jell-O, Kool-Aid Kool Pops, Popsicle, FrozFruit, and Life Savers, among others. Brands of **juice bars** include Dole Fruit 'n Juice, Fi-Bar, Chiquita, Minute Maid, Sunkist, and Welch's. Jell-O makes **gelatin pops,** and brands of **ice pops** include Popsicles, Jel Sert, and Good Humor.

cals=calories; fat=grams of fat; %fat=percent of calories from fat; sat=grams of saturated fat; sodium=milligrams of sodium

cookies, cakes, pies

Cookies
The range of cookie choices hasn't expanded as much as the ranges for other sweets, such as frozen desserts, but there are some leaner cookies available.

things that affect the fat content:
addition of chocolate: the presence of chocolate chips or a chocolate coating will increase the amount of fat

flavoring with nuts or peanut butter: the presence of these

also raises the fat level—pecan shortbread has 2 more grams of fat per serving than plain shortbread

creme filling: this usually contains more fat than the cookie dough it displaces

fruit filling: the more fruit in the cookie, the less fat—a fig newton, for instance, is one of the leanest cookies available

the fattiest . . .

food (30-gram serving)	cals	fat (g)	fat (%)	sat (g)	sodium (mg)
higher-fat chocolate chip cookies	170-215	11-13	50-56	2-4	105-195
higher-fat Pepperidge Farm cookies	155-195	10-13	48-60	2-4	50-85
pecan shortbread cookies	150-195	10-11	50-64	2	30-160

Higher-fat chocolate chip cookies include Chips Ahoy! and Keebler Deluxe brands. **Higher-fat Pepperidge Farm cookies** include Tahiti, Orleans Sandwich, and Brownie Chocolate Nut. **Shortbread** is, as its name suggests, prepared with more shortening than other cookies. **Pecan shortbread,** such as Keebler's Pecan Sandies, contains more fat than plain shortbread.

the less fatty . . .

food (30-gram serving)	cals	fat (g)	fat (%)	sat (g)	sodium (mg)
shortbread	150-175	7-9	43-51	1-2	65-150
peanut butter cookies	135-170	6-9	39-60	1-3	95-160

food (30-gram serving)	cals	fat (g)	fat (%)	sat (g)	sodium (mg)
sandwich: chocolate, vanilla, peanut butter	135-195	6-9	34-51	1-6	80-200
medium-fat chocolate chip	120-175	5-9	34-53	1-4	50-155
chocolate-covered graham crackers	105-195	5-9	35-54	2	65-150
wafers with creme filling	130-195	4-9	26-51	1-4	5-235
vanilla wafers	130-150	4-8	30-49	1-2	5-125
sugar cookies	140-160	6-9	40-48	1-4	70-150
oatmeal cookies	105-170	3-9	20-51	1-4	80-190

Oreos are an example of **chocolate sandwich cookies. Medium-fat chocolate chip cookie** brands include Keebler, McDonald's, Pepperidge Farm, Dunkin' Donuts, Archway, Chip-A-Roos, Almost Home, Frookie, and Duncan Hines. **Chocolate-covered graham crackers** have about double the fat of plain grahams.

the leaner . . .

food (30-gram serving)	cals	fat (g)	fat (%)	sat (g)	sodium (mg)
chocolate-coated marshmallow cookies	120-140	4-6	28-45	1-2	45-55
fruit-filled cookies	120-130	3-5	25-38	0-1	75-105
butter cookies	140-150	5-6	32-36	3	55-105
ginger snaps	125-140	2-5	15-35	0-1	105-200
lower-fat sandwich cookies	150	5	33	1	135

food (30-gram serving)	cals	fat (g)	fat (%)	sat (g)	sodium (mg)
animal crackers	130-135	4	27-30	1-2	55-170
graham cookies and crackers	105-130	2-4	15-30	0-1	40-195
lower-fat shortbread	130	3	23	2	150
fig-filled cookies	100-130	2-3	15-26	0-1	65-130
ladyfingers	110	3	23	1	45

Marshmallow is fat-free, so **marshmallow cookies** such as Nabisco's Mallomars tend to be leaner, as are **fruit-filled cookies.** Keebler's Elfin Delights is a brand of **lower-fat sandwich cookies. Graham cookies** here include Nabisco's Teddy Grahams as well as conventional graham crackers. Weight Watchers sells a **lower-fat shortbread. Fig-filled cookies** include all the Nabisco Newton varieties, as well as similar cookies from other manufacturers. **Ladyfingers** are small sponge cakes made with little or no shortening.

the leanest . . .

food (30-gram serving)	cals	fat (g)	fat (%)	sat (g)	sodium (mg)
"lite" animal crackers, chocolate chip, graham, or oatmeal cookies	120-130	2	15-16	0-1	140-180
fat-free fruit-filled, graham, or oatmeal cookies	70-130	0	0	0	45-155

"Lite" animal crackers and **lite graham snacks** include Keebler's Elfin Delights. **"Lite" chocolate chip cookies** and **fat-free graham snacks** are Nabisco's Snackwell brand.

"Lite" oatmeal cookies are made by Entenmann's and Nabisco's Snackwell, and **fat-free oatmeal cookies** are available from Frookie and Health Valley brands. Nature's Warehouse and Health Valley make **fat-free fruit-filled cookies,** and Nabisco makes **fat-free Fig Newtons.**

fat-skimming tips:
- pass up the shortbread and deluxe chocolate chip cookies

- look for old favorites: animal crackers, graham crackers, and fig-filled cookies

- try some of the new lower-fat or even fat-free brands of cookies

cals=calories; fat=grams of fat; %fat=percent of calories from fat; sat=grams of saturated fat; sodium=milligrams of sodium

Cakes
There is now a range of cakes available to choose, from rich cheesecakes to lower-fat fruit or chocolate cakes, even to fat-free pound cakes.

things that affect the fat content:
cheese: since cheese is one of the fattiest foods available, the presence of cheese in cake will increase its fat content

addition of icing or frosting: this increases the fat content since frosting contains more fat than cake

layers in the cake: cake with layers separated by icing will usually have more fat because the icing is usually fattier than the cake

flavoring with chocolate: chocolate cake and chocolate icing usually have more fat than white or yellow cake and white or yellow frosting

pudding versus conventional cakes: these contain more fat than conventional mixes

NOTE: The new official serving sizes for cakes are: 125 grams (about 4.5 ounces) for heavy cakes like cheesecake or fruitcake; 55 grams (about 2 ounces) for light cakes such as angel food or sponge cake without icing or filling; and 80 grams (about 2.8 ounces) for all other cakes. The following is based on these serving sizes.

the fattiest . . .

food (one serving)	cals	fat (g)	fat (%)	sat (g)	sodium (mg)
higher-fat cheesecake	375-445	23-33	52-66	12-18	180-355

These **higher-fat cheesecakes** are the kind available in restaurants.

the less fatty . . .

food (one serving)	cals	fat (g)	fat (%)	sat (g)	sodium (mg)
pound cake	315-370	14-20	41-48	4-9	220-430
medium-fat cheesecake	310-360	9-18	27-49	5-10	170-475
carrot cake, iced	280-300	16-18	47-55		285-315
chocolate layer cake	280-315	14-18	45-59		165-295
pineapple upside-down cake	400	15	34	4	400

pudding cake	275-290	12-15	38-48	2-4	265-420
fruitcake	405-450	11-14	25-29	1-2	180-335
frosted cake prepared from mix	210-305	10-14	35-43	2-4	180-275

Traditional **pound cake** was made with a pound of butter, a pound of eggs, a pound of shortening, and a pound of cake flour. Today, enough of the original recipe is retained to make it one of the richest available, such as Sara Lee's All Butter Pound Cake, which has 20 grams of fat per serving. However, there are now some "lite" versions (see section on "the leanest").

Sara Lee Original Plain Cream Cheesecake and Pepperidge Farm's American Collection Dessert cheesecake are examples of **medium-fat cheesecake. Pudding cakes** are available from Betty Crocker. Putting **frosting on a cake prepared from a cake mix** increases the fat content by 4 to 5 grams.

the leaner . . .

food (one serving)	cals	fat (g)	fat (%)	sat (g)	sodium (mg)
shortcake	215-275	9-11	37-38	3	100-405
medium-fat chocolate cake	170-215	6-10	30-43		95-295
cake prepared from mix, without frosting	245	6-9	23-35	1-2	380-455
gingerbread	245	8	30	2	365
lower-fat cheesecake	190-280	3-6	12-24	1-3	80-325

Sara Lee Double Chocolate Three Layer Cake and Weight Watchers Chocolate Cake are examples of **medium-fat**

chocolate cakes. Weight Watchers makes **lower-fat cheesecake.**

the leanest . . .

food (one serving)	cals	fat (g)	fat (%)	sat (g)	sodium (mg)
"lite" fruit or carrot cake	155-190	5	21-30		45-105
lower-fat chocolate cake	170-185	3-4	18-20		155-180
sponge cake	120-160	1-2	8-13	0-1	95-135
fat-free cake	185-255	0	0	0	230-385
angel food cake	140-145	0	1-2	0	100-415

"Lite" fruit or carrot cakes, including lemon cake and strawberry shortcake, are available from Sara Lee and Weight Watchers. Weight Watchers also sells **lower-fat chocolate cake.** Entenmann's, Pepperidge Farm, and Sara Lee make **fat-free cakes,** including fat-free pound cake. **Sponge cake** is prepared without shortening, and **angel food cake** uses egg whites instead of whole eggs, so both of these are reliable, leaner choices.

fat-skimming tips:
- go easy on the cheese, chocolate, and icing

- try sponge or angel food cake

- look for lower-fat and fat-free cakes

cals=calories; fat=grams of fat; %fat=percent of calories from fat; sat=grams of saturated fat; sodium=milligrams of sodium

Pies

Even among pies there are now some leaner alternatives available.

things that affect the fat content:
fried versus baked: many fried snack pies contain close to twice the amount of fat of regular baked pies

flavoring with nuts, coconut, chocolate, or cream: these ingredients raise the fat content of pies

this doesn't affect the fat content:
type of fruit: this makes little difference in the fat content

the fattiest . . .

food (one 125-gram or 4.5 oz. serving)	cals	fat (%)	fat (g)	sat (mg)	chol (mg)	sodium
higher-fat fried snack pies	390-500	21-29	45-52	3-10	0-20	475-480
pecan pie	345-510	17-23	35-45	3-5	40-50	265-535
chocolate pie	330-440	19-22	45-54	4-10	60	120-580
coconut cream pie	360-390	15-22	38-58	5-13	70	195-415

Hostess is a brand of **higher-fat fried snack pies,** some of which are the fattiest pies you can buy. Pecans are one of the fattiest nuts, so it figures that **pecan pie** would have some of the most fat.

the less fatty . . .

food (one-125 gram or 4.5 oz. serving)	cals	fat (g)	fat (%)	sat (g)	chol (mg)	sodium (mg)
coconut custard pie	255-345	13-20	45-51	6-7	45-70	265-425
banana, lemon, or strawberry cream pies	315-365	17-19	43-50	5-9	65	195-365
apple pie	290-370	12-19	28-49	2-4	0	215-375
berry, cherry, peach pies	270-360	10-15	26-45	2-4	0	235-465
mincemeat	300-365	11-15	33-45	2-3	0	320-490

Banquet and Pet-Ritz brands are examples of **cream pies** and **fruit pies**.

the leaner . . .

food (one 125-gram or 4.5 oz. serving)	cals	fat (g)	fat (%)	sat (g)	chol (mg)	sodium (mg)
pumpkin pie	170-265	7-12	30-41	1-4	25-55	175-355
lemon meringue pie	310-340	9-11	26-30	1-2	60	185-190
Boston cream pie	320	11	30	3	45	185

Meringue is made with egg whites and sugar, so **meringue pie** is among the leaner choices.

the leanest . . .

food (one 125-gram or 4.5 oz. serving)	cals	fat (g)	fat (%)	sat (g)	chol (mg)	sodium (mg)
lower-fat mousse or cream pies	210-280	4-6	12-33	0	5-10	170-280
lower-fat fruit pies	125-265	3-8	13-26	1-2	0	110-250

Weight Watchers makes **lower-fat mousse** and **cream pies.**
Weight Watchers, Sara Lee Free & Light, and Mrs. Smith's
Smart Style are brands of **lower-fat fruit pies.**

fat-skimming tips:
  • avoid fried snack pies

  • opt for fruit, pumpkin, mincemeat, and meringue pies
    over many of the nut, chocolate, and cream pies

  • try some of the new lower-fat pies

cals=calories; fat=grams of fat; %fat=percent of calories from fat; sat=grams of
saturated fat; sodium=milligrams of sodium

dairy and meat snacks

Spreadable Cheeses

Among the soft cheeses that can be spread on crackers, bagels,
and other foods, a broad range of choices for flavor and fat
content exists.

things that affect the fat content:
type of cheese: products made from real cheese contain more
fat than products made from process cheese spread or process
cheese product

  percent fat: each 10 percent increase in the amount of fat in
a Brie, Camembert, or similar cheese is the equivalent of 1 to
2 extra grams of fat per serving

this doesn't affect the fat content:
soft or whipped versus regular cream cheese: both have the
same amount of fat as regular cream cheese

the fattiest . . .

food (30-gram serving)	cals	fat (g)	fat (%)	sat (g)	chol (mg)	sodium (mg)
cream cheese	95-105	9-11	72-90	5-6	20-30	80-135
higher-fat cheese spreads	95-105	9-11	81-90	5-6	20-30	135-225

Cream cheese and **higher-fat cheese spreads** such as Rondeles and Alouette brands are the fattiest spreadable cheese commonly available. Cream cheese mixed with fruit may have slightly less fat than plain cream cheese.

the less fatty . . .

food (30-gram serving)	cals	fat (g)	fat (%)	sat (g)	chol (mg)	sodium (mg)
Camembert	90-120	6-10	60-80	5	25	195-295
cold pack cheese	95-120	8-9	63-70	3	20	180-225
Brie	95-105	8-9	69-80	5	25	195-355

The amount of fat in Brie and Camembert depends upon its percent fat. A brie labeled "50% fat" means that 50 percent of its *dry weight* consists of milkfat. That translates into about 28 percent fat, or 8 grams of fat per serving, in the product containing water that you buy. Camembert labeled "60% fat" is about 34 percent fat in the product you buy, or about 10 grams of fat per serving.

Cold pack cheese is one or more real cheeses that have been blended without heating.

the leaner . . .

food (30-gram serving)	cals	fat (g)	fat (%)	sat (g)	chol (mg)	sodium (mg)
cheese logs	95-100	6-8	60-63	3-5	15	270-280
squeezable cheese	85-90	6-8	66-79	4	15-20	365-545
Neufchâtel	65-85	5-8	75-90	3-4	15-25	105-180
medium-fat cheese spreads	65-95	4-8	30-90	2-4	10-20	130-160
"lite" cold pack cheese	75-85	4-5	51-56	2	15	215
"lite" cream cheese product	40-65	2-5	51-90	3	5-15	45-170

Squeezable cheese can be squirted out of a can or bottle. Nabisco's Easy Cheese and Squeeze-a-Snak are two examples. **Neufchâtel** is a fresh cheese similar to cream cheese and often used as a substitute for cream cheese. **Medium-fat cheese spreads** include Kraft Crockery, Cheez Whiz, and Shedd's Country Crock. Kraft Spreadery is a brand of **"lite" cold pack cheese.** Philadelphia and Weight Watchers are two brands of **"lite" cream cheese product.**

the leanest . . .

food (30-gram serving)	cals	fat (g)	fat (%)	sat (g)	chol (mg)	sodium (mg)
fat-free cream cheese	25-30	0		0	0	0-5	175-215

Philadelphia and Healthy Choice both make **fat-free cream cheese.**

fat-skimming tip:
   • try the lower-fat versions of cream cheese, spreadable

cheeses, or cold pack cheese—these contain one-half or less the fat of the fattier spreads

see these pages for:
83 hard cheeses
86 process cheeses

cals=calories; fat=grams of fat; %fat=percent of calories from fat; sat=grams of saturated fat; sodium=milligrams of sodium

Dips and Salsa
You can make or buy dips for chips, crackers, and vegetables that range from very fatty to fat-free.

things that affect the fat content:
conventional salad dressing versus dips: full-fat salad dressings contain more fat than most dips

sour cream versus other base: sour cream is fattier than most other ingredients used to make dips

bacon or cheese: these increase the fat content

this doesn't affect the fat content:
flavoring with clam, onion, or shrimp: these flavors contain little or no fat

the fattiest . . .

food (2T or 1 oz.)	cals	fat (g)	fat (%)	sat (g)	chol (mg)	sodium (mg)
full-fat blue cheese /ranch dressing	120-200	12-20	80-100	2-4	5-20	200-280
high-fat vegetable dips	135-140	14	90-94	0-4	20	0-110

Full-fat salad dressings used as vegetable dips contain much
more fat than most conventional dips. Marzetti's is an example of **high-fat vegetable dips.**

the less fatty . . .

food (2T or 1 oz.)	cals	fat (g)	fat (%)	sat (g)	chol (mg)	sodium (mg)
bacon dips	50-70	5-6	75-90	3	15-25	115-270
cheese dips	45-70	3-6	60-77	2-3	5-15	90-295
hummus	110	5	41	1	0	
onion dips	40-60	4-5	60-90	1-3	0-25	115-240
guacamole	45-50	4	72-80	1-2	0	120-210
most dips (clam, ranch, vegetable)	30-70	4	60-90	1-3	10-20	120-250

Hummus is a bean spread made with chickpeas and sesame
paste. Guacamole is a spread made with avocados, which contain a relatively large amount of fat for a vegetable or fruit.
Most popular dips, such as onion or clam, have about 4
grams of fat in a serving.

the leanest . . .

food (2T or 1 oz.)	cals	fat (g)	fat (%)	sat (g)	chol (mg)	sodium (mg)
low-fat and non-fat creamy dips	20-30	0-2	0-64	0-1	0-5	150-170
whole-milk yogurt	20	1	48	1	5	15
bean dips	25-40	0-1	0-30	0-1	0-5	55-180
non-fat salad dressings	10-30	0	0	0	0	240-420
salsa	5-15	0	0	0	0	60-310

Guiltless Gourmet, Slender Choice, and Heluva Good are brands of **low-fat and non-fat creamy dips.** Even **whole milk yogurt** used as a dip contains less fat than those made with sour cream. **Bean dips,** such as Hain and Frito-Lay brands, are low-fat because beans are very lean to begin with. **Non-fat salad dressings** can also be used as a dip for vegetables. Because **salsas** are made from fat-free ingredients like tomatoes, peppers, and spices, they make a readily available and popular non-fat dip. Old El Paso, Frito-Lay, Kaukauna, and Wise are some national brands.

fat-skimming tips:
- try salsa instead of a creamy dip

- use a non-fat salad dressing

- use yogurt or "lite" sour cream to make creamy dips

see these pages for:
135 potato, corn, and tortilla chips
148 crackers
211 salad dressing

cals=calories; fat=grams of fat; %fat=percent of calories from fat; sat=grams of saturated fat; sodium=milligrams of sodium

Puddings, Custards, and Gelatins
Puddings and custards are made with milk, and since the fat from milk is easily avoided, there are some low-fat and fat-free choices.

this affects the fat content:
type of milk used: for puddings and custards made at home, this determines the fat content more than anything else, but

ready-to-eat puddings made from skim milk can have as much fat as those made from whole milk

things that do not affect the fat content:
choice of flavors: most of these are concocted from synthetic, fat-free ingredients

pudding versus tapioca versus junket: these are all similar in fat content when prepared with the same kind of milk

the fattiest . . .

food (half-cup serving)	cals	fat (g)	fat (%)	sat (g)	chol (mg)	sodium (mg)
pudding sundaes and swirls	170-220	6-7	29-32	2	5	130-180
higher-fat ready-to-eat puddings	160-190	6-7	30-33	1-2	5	115-200
parfaits	170-180	6	30-32	1	0	150-200

Most **higher-fat ready-to-eat puddings** are not made from whole milk, but they contain the same amount of fat as if they were. That's because these puddings are manufactured from skim milk and partially hydrogenated vegetable oil. Brands are Swiss Miss, Hunt's Snack Pack, and Jell-O. **Pudding sundaes and swirls,** such as Swiss Miss and Jell-O brands, have extra fat added.

the less fatty . . .

food (half-cup serving)	cals	fat (g)	fat (%)	sat (g)	chol (mg)	sodium (mg)
mousse made with whole milk	100-150	4-6	33-39	0-2	10	50-110

food (half-cup serving)	cals	fat (g)	fat (%)	sat (g)	chol (mg)	sodium (mg)
pudding made with whole milk	155-180	4-6	20-35	3-4	15	145-480
custard made with whole milk	120-165	4-5	28-30	3	80	125-200
junket, tapioca, flan with whole milk	110-190	4-5	19-30	1-3	5-20	65-190

These foods have similar amounts of fat when prepared with whole milk.

the leaner . . .

food (half-cup serving)	cals	fat (g)	fat (%)	sat (g)	chol (mg)	sodium (mg)
"lite" mousse	70	3	39	2	0	50-105
pudding made with 2% milk	145-160	2-3	11-19	1-2	0-10	150-420
junket or flan made with 2% milk	100-135	2-3	15-23	1-2	0-10	60-195
"lite" ready-to-eat pudding	100	1-2	9-20	0	0	105-120

Weight Watchers and Estee make **"lite" mousse mixes.** Hunt's Light Snack Pack and Swiss Miss Light are two **"lite" ready-to-eat puddings.**

the leanest . . .

food (half-cup serving)	cals	fat (g)	fat (%)	sat (g)	chol (mg)	sodium (mg)
fat-free ready-to-eat puddings	100	0	0	0	0	170-200
gelatin desserts, regular	75-80	0	0	0	0	0-130

food (half-cup serving)	cals	fat (g)	fat (%)	sat (g)	chol (mg)	sodium (mg)
"lite" pudding made with skim milk	60-70	0	0	0	0	65-70
"lite" gelatin desserts	10	0	0	0	0	0-100

Hershey's Free and Jell-O Free are **fat-free ready-to-eat puddings. Gelatin desserts,** such as Jell-O and Royal brands, are made from fat-free animal protein. The regular kind is sweetened with sugar, the **"lite" gelatin desserts** with aspartame. **"Lite" pudding** is also sweetened with aspartame.

fat-skimming tips:
- gelatin desserts are fat-free, so choose them in restaurants when you don't know the fat amounts in other desserts

- make puddings, custards, and other milk-based desserts with skim or low-fat milk

cals=calories; fat=grams of fat; %fat=percent of calories from fat; sat=grams of saturated fat; sodium=milligrams of sodium

Meat and Cheese Snacks: Jerky, Salami, and String Cheese

Popular snack foods made of meat or cheese can be fatty, so know your products.

this affects the fat content:

sausage versus jerky: mixtures of meat and fat with a sausage-like texture contain more fat than slices of dried, fibrous meat like beef jerky

the fattiest . . .

food (30-gram serving)	cals	fat (g)	fat (%)	sat (g)	chol (mg)	sodium (mg)
meat sticks and meat snacks	100-200	9-17	66-83	6	25-40	385-575
pepperoni	140-150	12-14	76-84	5-6		560
summer sausage sticks	145	13	82	5		535

Meat sticks, meat snacks, pepperoni, and summer sausage sticks are mixtures of meat and fat similar to pork or Polish sausage, except that ounce for ounce these contain more fat and less water. Slim Jim and Pemmican are two brands.

the less fatty . . .

food (30-gram serving)	cals	fat (g)	fat (%)	sat (g)	chol (mg)	sodium (mg)
hard salami	105-130	9-11	72-82	4	25	560
Vienna sausage	85	8	80	3	15	285

Hard salami has less fat than pepperoni because it contains more water. **Vienna sausages** are basically tiny hot dogs, with more water than hard salami.

the leaner . . .

food (30-gram serving)	cals	fat (g)	fat (%)	sat (g)	chol (mg)	sodium (mg)
pickled sausage	80-90	6-7	68-76	2-3		440-470
string cheese	85-95	6-7	60-68	4	15-20	160-235
beef jerky	85-135	2-7	23-45	0-2	25-35	455-985

String cheese is essentially mozzarella cheese. **Beef jerky** has less fat than meat sticks, pepperoni, or salami because it does not contain ground-up beef or pork fat.

the leanest . . .

food (30-gram serving)	cals	fat (g)	fat (%)	sat (g)	chol (mg)	sodium (mg)
pickled pig's knuckles	50	4	65	2	—	420
pickled pig's feet	40	3	61	1	—	510
"lite" string cheese	45-65	0-3	0-45	0-2	10	215-250

Pig's knuckles and **pig's feet** contain more connective tissue and less muscle and fat than sticks, snacks, sausage, and jerky. **"Lite" string cheese** is available from Polly-O and Healthy Choice.

fat–skimming tip:
- snack on hard salami, which is leaner than pepperoni, meat sticks, or meat snacks, and on beef jerky, which is leaner still

cals=calories; fat=grams of fat; %fat=percent of calories from fat; sat=grams of saturated fat; sodium=milligrams of sodium

fruit

Fresh Fruit

Fresh fruit is virtually fat-free, so the calories are what differ the most among your choices.

this affects the calorie content:

water content: the proportion of water in a fruit, more than anything else, determines its calorie content: the less water, the more sugar and calories; the more water, the less room for sugar and calories

those with the most calories . . .

food (one-cup serving)	cals	fat (g)	fat (%)	sat (g)	sodium (mg)
higher-calorie fruit: bananas	205	1	5	0	0

Bananas are the densest fruit, hence they have the most calories.

those with fewer calories . . .

food (one-cup serving)	cals	fat (g)	fat (%)	sat (g)	sodium (mg)
medium-calorie fruits	90-115	0-1	4-12	0	0-5

Medium-calorie fruits include mangoes, sweet cherries, pears, and plums.

those with even fewer calories . . .

food (one-cup serving)	cals	fat (g)	fat (%)	sat (g)	sodium (mg)
lower-calorie fruits	60-85	0-1	1-12	0	0-15

Lower-calorie fruits include apples, tangerines, oranges, guavas, blueberries, sour cherries, pineapple, grapefruit, blackberries, apricots, peaches, nectarines, currants, raspberries, honeydew melon, and grapes.

those with the least calories . . .

food (one-cup serving)	cals	fat (g)	fat (%)	sat (g)	sodium (mg)
lowest-calorie fruits	45-55	0-1	3-11	0	0-20

The lowest-calorie fruits include cantaloupe, papaya, watermelon, cranberries, casaba melon, and strawberries. Melons and strawberries contain the most water, so they have the least amount of calories.

fat-skimming tip:
  • fruits are non-fat and relatively low-calorie, so use them to keep dishes lower in fat and calories

see these pages for:
  199 canned and frozen fruits
  161 fruit snacks

cals=calories; fat=grams of fat; %fat=percent of calories from fat; sat=grams of saturated fat; sodium=milligrams of sodium

Canned and Frozen Fruit
Since fruit is virtually fat-free, the calories are what differ most among the choices.

this affects the calorie content:
canning liquid: fruit canned in *heavy* syrup contains about 50 more calories per serving than fruit canned in *light* syrup; fruit canned in light syrup contains about 25 more calories than fruit canned in *juice*; fruit canned in juice contains about 50 more calories than fruit canned in *water*.

the choices . . .

food (one-cup serving)	cals	fat (g)	fat (%)	sat (g)	sodium (mg)
fruit canned in heavy syrup	185-245	0	0	0	0-50
applesauce, sweetened	195	0	0	0	10
frozen strawberries	145-190	0	0	0	10
fruit canned in light syrup	130-190	0	0	0	0-50
fruit canned in juice	110-150	0	0	0	5-20
fruit canned in water	60-130	0	0	0	0-10
unsweetened or "lite" applesauce	100-105	0	0	0	5-20

A cup of fruit canned in heavy syrup will contain at least twice the calories of fruit canned in water. **"Lite" applesauce** is sweetened with aspartame rather than sugar.

see these pages for:
    197 fresh fruit
    161 fruit snacks

cals=calories; fat=grams of fat; %fat=percent of calories from fat; sat=grams of saturated fat; sodium=milligrams of sodium

➤ FLAVORINGS, SAUCES, DRESSINGS, AND CONDIMENTS

dairy- and oil-based
butter, margarine, and vegetable oil spreads
vegetable oils
mayonnaise and mayonnaise-like dressings
salad dressings
grated cheese
sour creams

sweet flavorings
sugar, sugar substitutes, and other sweeteners
jam, jelly, preserves, honey, and other sweet spreads
pancake syrups and toppings
dessert toppings: syrups, sweet toppings, and whipped creams

sauces
catsup, barbecue sauce, and other meat or seafood sauces
mustard and other hot or spicy sauces
gravy

condiments
pickles, olives, peppers, and chilies
relishes

dairy- and oil-based

Butter, Margarine, and Vegetable Oil Spreads

Butter, margarine, and vegetable oil spreads are a leading source of fat in the American diet. The introduction of vegetable oil spreads, all of which contain less fat than margarine, makes it possible to select products either slightly or significantly lower in fat—if you know what to look for among the bewildering variety of choices now available.

things that affect the fat content:
percent of vegetable oil in margarine or spread: this determines the amount of fat—margarine is 80 percent, spreads are anywhere from 0 percent to 75 percent—the percents are specified on the front of the package labels

whipping: whipping butter and margarine dilutes them with air, so whipped butters and margarine contain less fat

things that do not affect the fat content:
type of oil in margarine or spreads: all oils used to make mar-

garine contain the same amount of fat, so whether the product is made from corn, canola, or another oil doesn't affect the *total fat content*—but it can affect the *saturated fat content* by 1 to 2 grams per serving

stick versus tub versus squeezable: the form of the margarine or spread doesn't affect the total fat content, but the fat in softer products is likely to be less saturated

the fattiest . . .

food (one tablespoon)	cals	fat (g)	fat (%)	sat (g)	chol (mg)	sodium (mg)
butter	100	11	100	6	30	120
margarine	100	11	100	1-3	0	0-170
blends of butter and margarine	100	11	100	2-3	10-15	0-120

Butter and **margarine** contain the same amount of calories and fat because they both consist of 80 percent fat and 20 percent water by weight. The fat in butter is milkfat, which is highly saturated, whereas the fat in margarine is vegetable oil, which may be partly saturated by manufacturers to make it solid at room temperature. **Blends,** such as Land O' Lakes Country Morning, are mixtures of margarine and butter intended to provide some of the taste of butter along with the healthier fat of margarine.

the less fatty . . .

food (one tablespoon)	cals	fat (g)	fat (%)	sat (g)	chol (mg)	sodium (mg)
spreads of 70%-75% oil	90	10	100	1-2	0	70-110
spreads of 64%-68% oil	80	9	100	1-3	0	0-115
spreads of 60% oil	80	8	100	1-2	0	70-110
spreads of 48%-53% oil	60	7	100	1-2	0	0-130
whipped butter	70	7	100	5	15	65-70
whipped margarine	70	7	100	1-2	0	0-70

Vegetable oil spreads consist of less vegetable oil and more water than margarine. Some of them, such as the 64 percent to 75 percent vegetable oil spreads, are not all that different in calories and fat from margarine because margarine is, in essence, an 80 percent vegetable oil spread. Whipping reduces the fat by about a third in servings of **whipped butter** or **whipped margarine.**

the leaner . . .

food (one tablespoon)	cals	fat (g)	fat (%)	sat (g)	chol (mg)	sodium (mg)
spreads of 40%-48% oil	50	6	100	1-3	0	0-140
spreads of 30% oil	45	4	100	1	0	75
spreads of 17% oil	20	3	100	0	0	0-110

To find a spread with no more than half the fat of butter or margarine, look for products consisting of **40 percent or less vegetable oil.** However, since these spreads are mostly water, they are not suitable for use in certain types of cooking because they will spatter. Look for the warnings on the labels.

the leanest . . .

food (one tablespoon or one serving)	cals	fat (g)	fat (%)	sat (g)	chol (mg)	sodium (mg)
honey butter	50	1	18	0	5	5
fat-free margarine	5	0	0	0	0	95
powdered "butter" products (one serving)	5	0	0	0	0	65-85

Honey butter is honey with a very small amount of butter blended in. New **fat-free margarines,** such as Promise Ultra, are basically water, flavors, and additives. **Powdered "butter" products,** such as Molly McButter and Butter Buds, are flakes or grains of salt, seasoning, and dairy flavor extracts.

TIP: When manufacturers harden vegetable oil to make margarines or spreads, they create a special kind of fat called **trans fatty acids.** Unfortunately, these raise cholesterol levels just like saturated fats do. To avoid trans fatty acids in margarin or spreads, **choose softer products,** such as squeezable or tub varieties instead of sticks, or **fat-free margarine.** Alternatively, **use a cooking spray** and **substitute vegetable oil** when you can for margarine or butter.

fat-skimming tips:
- look for the products with the lowest percent of vegetable oil, remembering that margarine is 80 percent oil

- try whipped butter or margarine

- use a cooking spray when you can

- try honey butter

see this page for:
  207 vegetable oils

cals=calories; fat=grams of fat; %fat=percent of calories from fat; sat=grams of
saturated fat; sodium=milligrams of sodium

Vegetable Oils

Vegetable oils are the leading source of fat in the American diet
because they are used so much in food manfacturing and by
restaurants. Among foods that Americans buy and use in their
homes, vegetable oils rank as the thirteenth leading source of fat.

this doesn't affect the fat content:
type of oil: all vegetable oils contain the same amount of fat—
they differ only in how saturated the fat is

the fattiest . . .

food (one tablespoon)	cals	fat (g)	fat (%)	sat (g)	sodium (mg)
all vegetable oils	120	14	100	1-12	0

Vegetable oils are 100 percent fat. That's why they contain
more fat per tablespoon than butter and margarine, which are
"only" 80 percent fat and 20 percent water.

Where one vegetable oil differs from another is in how saturated the fat is, as follows:

saturated fat content of common oils in a one-tablespoon serving:

	sat (g)
corn, olive, peanut, soybean, sesame, sunflower	2
canola, sunflower, safflower, walnut	1

The one-gram-per-tablespoon difference in saturated fat between canola and soybean oils translates into a total of 48 less grams of saturated fat in a 24-ounce bottle of canola oil than in a 24-ounce bottle of soybean oil.

Here are the amounts of saturated fat found in a one-table-spoon serving of less commonly available vegetable oils:

saturated fat content of less common oils in a one-tablespoon serving:

	sat (g)
coconut	12
palm kernel	11
palm	7
cottonseed	4
rice bran, wheat germ	3
avocado	2
hazelnut	1

Coconut, palm kernel, and palm oils are the highly saturated "tropical" oils that food manufacturers have been pressured to remove from their products.

the less fatty . . .

food (one serving)	cals	fat (g)	fat (%)	sat (g)	sodium (mg)
cooking sprays	0-7	0-1	0-100	0	0

Cooking sprays, such as Pam or Mazola brands, are tiny droplets of emulsified vegetable oil that can be sprayed out in small amounts over a wide area, resulting in the use of less oil.

TIP: One of the advantages of vegetable oils over margarine is that oils are not partially hydrogenated or saturated, so they do not contain **trans fatty acids.** Trans fatty acids raise cholesterol levels like saturated fats do. So substitute vegetable oils for margarine or vegetable oil spreads when possible.

fat-skimming tip:
• use cooking sprays when possible

see this page for:
   203 butter, margarine, and vegetable oil spreads

cals=calories; fat=grams of fat; %fat=percent of calories from fat; sat=grams of saturated fat; sodium=milligrams of sodium

Mayonnaise and Mayonnaise-like Dressings

Mayonnaise and salad dressing have been an important source of fat in the American diet for a long time. But that may be changing because of the recent introduction of reduced-fat and even fat-free versions of these foods.

this affects the fat content:
mayonnaise versus salad dressing: by law, regular mayonnaise contains about 40 percent more fat than regular salad dressing

this does not affect the fat content:
type of oil: whether it's soybean, safflower, or another oil makes no difference to the *total* fat content and only a small difference in the *saturated* fat content

the fattiest . . .

food (one tablespoon)	cals	fat (g)	fat (%)	sat (g)	chol (mg)	sodium (mg)
real mayonnaise	100-110	11-12	90-100	1-2	5-10	0-100

Real mayonnaise consists of at least 65 percent vegetable oil by weight, along with vinegar and egg yolks. Despite the presence of eggs, a serving does not contain much cholesterol.

the less fatty . . .

food (one tablespoon)	cals	fat (g)	fat (%)	sat (g)	chol (mg)	sodium (mg)
salad dressing	70	7	90	1	5-10	85-100
lower-fat mayonnaise	40-60	3-6	68-90	0-1	0-10	35-160
lower-fat salad dressing	40-50	3-5	68-90	1	0-5	45-125

Salad dressing consists of at least 30 percent vegetable oil by weight, along with vinegar, starchy paste, and egg yolks. **Lower-fat mayonnaise** and **lower-fat salad dressing,** such as Kraft Light, Miracle Whip Light, Hellmann's, and Weight Watchers brands, contain less oil and more starchy paste and other thickeners. Once mayonnaise and salad dressing have had their fat content reduced, there is little nutritional difference between them.

the leaner . . .

food (one tablespoon)	cals	fat (g)	fat (%)	sat (g)	chol (mg)	sodium (mg)
mustard-mayonnaise blend	40	3	75	0	0	225
tofu mayonnaise	35	3	77	0	0	100

Hellmann's Dijonnaise is a brand of **mustard-mayonnaise** blend with more mustard than mayo, Golden Soy a brand of **tofu mayonnaise** made from soybeans.

the leanest . . .

food (one tablespoon)	cals	fat (g)	fat (%)	sat (g)	chol (mg)	sodium (mg)
fat-free salad dressing	10-15	0	0	0	0	105-190
fat-free mayonnaise	10	0	0	0	0	105-135

Fat-free salad dressing and **fat-free mayonnaise** are now readily available. Brands include Weight Watchers, Kraft Free, Miracle Whip Free, and Smart Beat.

fat-skimming tips:
- choose salad dressing over mayonnaise

- try fat-free mayonnaise or salad dressing

cals=calories; fat=grams of fat; %fat=percent of calories from fat; sat=grams of saturated fat; sodium=milligrams of sodium

Salad Dressings
Salad dressings used to be the major hazard at salad bars. Two tablespoons contained more fat than many steaks and undid many of the benefits of eating salad. But today, the ready availability of reduced-fat and fat-free dressings means that there is no excuse for eating full-fat salad dressings.

things that affect the fat content:
full-fat versus reduced-fat versus fat-free: this determines the fat content of salad dressing more than anything else

cheese or cream: dressings such as blue cheese or ranch are higher in fat than dressings made with tomatoes or relish such as French or Thousand Island

this doesn't affect the fat content:

creamy versus chunky: these terms don't always mean fattier, because it depends upon what the cream or chunks are made of

the fattiest . . .

food (two tablespoons)	cals	fat (g)	fat (%)	sat (g)	chol (mg)	sodium (mg)
full-fat salad dressings						
ranch	120-200	12-20	90-100	2-4	5-20	200-280
blue cheese	120-180	12-18	80-100	2-4	10-20	110-460
oil and vinegar	140-160	14-18	90-100	2	0	160-580
cucumber	140-160	16	90-100	2	5	380-420
cheese	140-160	14-16	90-100	2	10-20	230-340
Caesar	120-160	12-16	90-100	2	5-30	140-440
buttermilk	120-160	12-16	90-100	2	10	200-270
garlic	100-140	10-16	90-100	2	0	200-370
Italian	100-160	10-16	90-100	1-2	0-20	40-660
Thousand Island	100-140	10-14	75-90	1-2	10-20	160-310
vinaigrette	100-120	10-14	90-100	0-4	0-20	180-360
mustard	100-160	10-12	68-90	0-2	20	140-380
French	120-140	10-12	75-90	1-2	0-10	160-480
Russian	100-120	10	75-90	2	10	160-300

the less fatty . . .

food (two tablespoons)	cals	fat (g)	fat (%)	sat (g)	chol (mg)	sodium (mg)
reduced-fat salad dressings	40-120	1-10	13-100	0-2	0-20	130-600

Reduced-fat salad dressings, such as Hidden Valley Ranch Take Heart, Kraft, and Naturally Fresh brands, use thickeners to replace the fat. But some brands are much lighter than others, so it's necessary to read their nutrition labels to see just how much less fat the particular products contain.

the leanest . . .

food (two tablespoons)	cals	fat (g)	fat (%)	sat (g)	chol (mg)	sodium (mg)
fat-free salad dressings	10-40	0	0	0	0	0-600

There are now dozens of brands of **fat-free salad dressings** available, including Good Seasons Fat Free, Wish-Bone, Healthy Sensation, and Weight Watchers. Their one drawback is that many contain relatively large amounts of sodium contributed by some of the additives used to replace the fat.

fat-skimming tips:
   • look for fat-free salad dressing

   • look carefully at the labels of reduced-calorie dressings because there is wide variation in their fat contents

see this page for:
   65 salad fixings

cals=calories; fat=grams of fat; %fat=percent of calories from fat; sat=grams of saturated fat; sodium=milligrams of sodium

Grated Cheese
Now that pasta dishes are so popular, the use of grated cheese to top them is growing. Despite the increasing number of grated cheese products, they differ very little in fat.

things that affect the fat content:
amount of non-cheese ingredients: products made entirely
from one cheese or a blend of cheeses will contain more fat
than those products consisting of a mixture of cheese and
other non-cheese dairy ingredients.

type of milk: products made from skim milk cheese will
contain less fat than those made of whole milk

the fattiest . . .

food (one tablespoon)	cals	fat (g)	fat (%)	sat (g)	chol (mg)	sodium (mg)
Romano cheese	25	2	62	1	5	65
Parmesan cheese	20-25	2	59	1	5	80-95
blend of Parmesan and other cheeses	20-25	1-2	39-62	1	5	80-90

Romano cheese and **parmesan cheese** are similar in calorie and fat content.

the other choices . . .

food (one tablespoon)	cals	fat (g)	fat (%)	sat (g)	chol (mg)	sodium (mg)
grated American cheese food	25	1	48	1	5	160
Italian, pasta, or cheese toppings	10-20	1	36-53	0	0-5	55-80
"lite" grated cheese	15-20	1	36-39	0	0-5	75-95
imitation grated cheese	15	1	34	1	0	75
fat-free grated cheese	15	0	0	0	5	45-60

These choices differ very little. **Grated American cheese food** made by Kraft is process cheese food (see the section of process cheeses for an explanation of how this differs from process cheese). **Italian, pasta, or cheese toppings** consist of real cheese blended with other low- or non-fat milk ingredients such as casein or whey. These toppings cost less and contain less fat than 100 percent cheese. **Imitation grated cheese,** the kind served in some restaurants, is fabricated from vegetable oil instead of dairy fat. **Fat-free grated cheese,** such as Weight Watchers brand, is made with skim milk cheese.

fat-skimming tip:
* the differences are minor among the grated cheeses, so enjoy them in moderation

cals=calories; fat=grams of fat; %fat=percent of calories from fat; sat=grams of saturated fat; sodium=milligrams of sodium

Sour Creams and Alternatives
Sour cream has joined the parade of foods that have many brands of lower-fat and even fat-free alternatives available.

this affects the fat content:
cream versus half-and-half: half-and-half is a mixture of cream and milk, so soured half-and-half has less fat than pure soured cream

the fattiest . . .

food (two tablespoons)	cals	fat (g)	fat (%)	sat (g)	chol (mg)	sodium (mg)
sour cream	65	6	90	3-4	10-20	10

Sour cream is pasteurized dairy cream, containing at least 18 percent milkfat by weight, which has been soured by special bacteria.

the leaner . . .

food (two tablespoons)	cals	fat (g)	fat (%)	sat (g)	chol (mg)	sodium (mg)
sour topping	50-60	4-5	78-80	5	0	30
sour half-and-half	55	4	72	2	10	20
imitation sour cream	45	4	90	0	0	20
reduced-fat sour cream	25-55	2-4	45-72	0-2	5-10	15-145

Sour topping is a less expensive sour cream–like product manufactured from dairy ingredients and used by some restaurants. **Sour half-and-half** is soured half-and-half, which contains between 10.5 percent and 18 percent milkfat by weight compared to at least 18 percent in cream. **Imitation sour cream,** such as King brand, is made with vegetable oil instead of dairy fat. Brands of **reduced–fat sour cream** include Light 'n Lively and Dannon's Instead.

the leanest . . .

food (two tablespoons)	cals	fat (g)	fat (%)	sat (g)	chol (mg)	sodium (mg)
fat-free sour cream	30	0	0	0	10	40

Fat-free sour cream is manufactured from fat-free dairy ingredients, along with thickeners to replace the fat. Land O' lakes is a national brand.

see this page for:
  190 dips

cals=calories; fat=grams of fat; %fat=percent of calories from fat; sat=grams of saturated fat; sodium=milligrams of sodium

sweet flavorings

Sugar, Sugar Substitutes, and Other Sweeteners

Although sugar and other sweeteners consist of just calories and flavor with few nutrients, at least they're fat-free.

There are only trivial caloric differences among the various sugars and syrups. Only the sugar substitutes, such as aspartame and saccharin, are significantly different.

things that do not affect the calorie content:
color of sugar: the caramel coloring that makes white sugar brown does not add calories

natural versus wild, spun, or raw honey: they all have the same number of calories

blackstrap versus light, sulphured, or unsulphured molasses: none of these has a significantly different number of calories

the choices . . .

food (one teaspoon)	cals	fat (g)	fat (%)	sat (g)	sodium (mg)
molasses	15-25	0	0	0	5-20
honey	20	0	0	0	0
corn syrup	20	0	0	0	10
maple syrup	20	0	0	0	0
sugar	10-16	0	0	0	0
fructose	12	0	0	0	0
sugar substitutes	0-4	0	0	0	0-30

Each teaspoon of **sugar** provides 16 calories. A serving of **fructose** contains slightly fewer calories since it is sweeter than sucrose and less is needed. The **sugar substitutes** include aspartame, also known as Nutrasweet, which contains up to 4 calories per serving, and saccharin, which is calorie-free.

see this page for:
221 syrups

cals=calories; fat=grams of fat; %fat=percent of calories from fat; sat=grams of saturated fat; sodium=milligrams of sodium

Jam, Jelly, Preserves, Honey, and Other Sweet Spreads

Sweet spreads are fat-free. Only the calories differ among your choices, and the calories don't differ all that much.

things that do not affect the calorie content:
type of fruit: the fruits used to make these products are very similar in calorie content

fruit-juice sweetening: products using fruit juice instead of sugar for sweetening have only a few less calories per serving

natural versus wild, sun, or raw honey: all types of honey contain the same number of calories

the choices . . .

food (one tablespoon)	cals	fat (g)	fat (%)	sat (g)	sodium (mg)
honey	65	0	0	0	0
jam, preserves, jelly, marmalade	50-55	0	0	0	5-10

food (one tablespoon)	cals	fat (g)	fat (%)	sat (g)	sodium (mg)
fruit spreads	40	0	0	0	0-10
fruit butters	30-35	0	0	0	0-5
"lite" marmalade, jelly, preserves	20-25	0	0	0	0-15

As you can see, the calories do not differ greatly among the choices. **Honey** is the most concentrated, so it contains the most calories. **Jams, preserves, jelly, and marmalade** all contain about the same proportion of fruit to sugar, so they have the same amount of calories. **Fruit spreads** and **"lite" marmalade, jelly, and preserves** are made with more pectin or other thickeners and less sweetener, so they contain fewer calories. **Fruit butters** contain more pulp and thus less sugar than jam, preserves, jelly, and marmalade.

fat-skimming tip:
  • these sweet, non-fat spreads make good substitutes for high-fat spreads such as peanut butter, cream cheese, butter, margarine, or vegetable oil spreads

cals=calories; fat=grams of fat; %fat=percent of calories from fat; sat=grams of saturated fat; sodium=milligrams of sodium

Pancake Syrups and Toppings
These foods are fat-free (with one small exception), so only the calories differ among your choices.

things that affect the fat or calorie content:
addition of butter: pancake syrups containing a small amount of butter added for flavor have fat; other syrups don't

fruit versus sugar syrups: fruit syrups are less concentrated than sugar syrups, so they contain fewer calories

things that do not affect the calorie content:
table versus pancake versus waffle syrup: these are all names for the same basic syrup

type of sugar: cane, maple, corn, and sorghum syrups all have about the same calorie content

light versus dark color: dark means only that dark substances such as caramel have been retained or added

the choices . . .

food (2 tablespoons)	cals	fat (g)	fat (%)	sat (g)	sodium (mg)
pancake syrup flavored with butter	120	1	5	0	40
pancake, table, or waffle syrups	105-130	0	0	0	25-40
sorghum syrup	120	0	0	0	5
corn syrup, light or dark	110	0	0	0	50-60
maple syrup	105	0	0	0	5
pourable fruit syrups	70	0	0	0	25
"lite" syrup	30-60	0	0	0	35-115

There are only small differences among these syrups, which include brands such as Mrs. Butterworth's, Karo, Aunt Jemima, and King. **Pourable fruit syrups** are available from Polaner. Brands of **"lite" syrup,** which uses thickeners to replace sugar syrup, include Hungry Jack, Log Cabin, and Empress.

fat-skimming tip:
   • syrup is always a better topping for pancakes, waffles, and French toast than butter or margarine

see these pages for:
   17 pancakes
   20 waffles and French toast
   203 butter, margarine, and vegetable oil spreads

cals=calories; fat=grams of fat; %fat=percent of calories from fat; sat=grams of saturated fat; sodium=milligrams of sodium

Dessert Toppings: Syrups, Sweet Toppings, and Whipped Creams

Many of the sweet syrups and toppings, as well as whipped creams to put on ice cream, are not that high in fat—if you know what to look for.

things that affect the fat content:
toppings that harden: dessert toppings that harden after heating do so in part because they contain extra fat, particularly saturated fat

   syrup versus topping: syrups are usually leaner than many of the thicker toppings

   hot versus cold toppings: toppings designed to be heated before pouring usually contain more fat than toppings not designed to be heated

   fudge versus chocolate toppings: fudge toppings frequently contain more fat than chocolate-flavored toppings because fudge is prepared with extra butter or other fat

   nuts: nuts usually raise the fat content of syrups and toppings

this doesn't affect the fat content:
packaging of whipped toppings: toppings frozen in containers, pressurized in cans, or from dry mixes all have similar amounts of fat and calories

the fattiest . . .

food (2 tablespoons)	cals	fat (g)	fat (%)	sat (g)	sodium (mg)
dessert toppings that harden	190-200	15-16	71-72	4	25-50

Dessert toppings that harden when they are heated and poured over ice cream are manufactured with large amounts of highly saturated vegetable oil, because saturated fats become solid at room temperature. Smucker's "magic shell" toppings are one brand.

the less fatty . . .

food (2 tablespoons)	cals	fat (g)	fat (%)	sat (g)	sodium (mg)
higher-fat sweet toppings	100-160	3-5	17-38		30-100
nuts and syrup toppings	130-150	1-4	7-30	0-1	120
heavy whipped cream	25	3	96	2	5

Brands of **higher-fat sweet toppings,** which are often hot fudge, hot caramel, or hot butterscotch flavor, include Smucker's, Hershey's, and Kraft. **Heavy whipped cream** is prepared from heavy cream, which is at least 36 percent milk-fat by weight.

the leaner . . .

food (2 tablespoons)	cals	fat (g)	fat (%)	sat (g)	sodium (mg)
whipped toppings:					
frozen whipped topping	25-30	1-2	38-64	0-1	0
light whipped cream	20	2	95	1	5
whipped cream or topping, pressurized can	15-20	1-2	72-90	0-2	5-10
low-fat whipped topping, mix	10-20	0-2	0-100	0-1	0-10
"lite" frozen whipped topping	15	1	56	0	0
sweet toppings:					
lower-fat dessert topping	90-140	0-1	0-9	0-1	15-145
chocolate syrup	110-130	0	0	0	20-35
fruit syrup topping	70-130	0	0	0	0-25
"lite" hot topping	70	0	0	0	35

Frozen whipped toppings and **"lite" frozen whipped toppings,** such as Cool Whip and Cook Whip Lite, are made from soybeans. **Light whipped cream** is prepared from light cream, which consists of 30 percent to 36 percent milkfat. Brands of **whipped cream** or **dairy topping in a pressurized can** include Reddi-Whip and Kemps. Dream Whip is a national brand of **whipped topping mix** prepared with milk.

Lower-fat dessert toppings include Evans brand and some Smucker's products. Smucker's also makes a **"lite" fudge topping. Chocolate syrup,** such as Hershey's brand, and **fruit syrup toppings,** such as Polaner, Smucker's, and Evans brands, consist of sugar, water, and flavors, but no fat.

fat-skimming tips:
• pass up the toppings that harden and those with nuts.

• choose chocolate syrup or fruit syrup toppings

see this page for:
166 ice cream

cals=calories; fat=grams of fat; %fat=percent of calories from fat; sat=grams of saturated fat; sodium=milligrams of sodium

---

sauces

Catsup, Barbecue Sauce, and Other Meat or Seafood Sauces
Most of the sauces intended to complement the flavor of meat, seafood, and other foods are low in fat. A few, however, are worth avoiding.

this affects the fat content:
oil, butter, or margarine base versus tomato base: higher-fat sauces are prepared from vegetable oil, butter, or margarine, whereas lower-fat sauces are most frequently prepared from tomatoes

this doesn't affect the fat content:
various sweet, spicy, or smoked flavors: honey, mustard, sweet and sour, mesquite, and other flavors of barbecue, dipping, and similar sauces have nothing to do with the fat content

the fattiest . . .

food (two tablespoons)	cals	fat (g)	fat (%)	sat (g)	sodium (mg)
tartar sauce	100-260	10-20	90-100	1-4	120-380

The major ingredient in **tartar sauce** is vegetable oil. Alternatives are "lite" tartar sauces with one-fourth this much fat, or seafood cocktail sauces with no fat at all.

the less fatty . . .

food (two tablespoons)	cals	fat (g)	fat (%)	sat (g)	sodium (mg)
béarnaise sauce	60-95	5-9	75-88	5	160

Béarnaise sauce is a rich meat sauce prepared with milk and butter or margarine. Commercial brands include Knorr and McCormick/Schilling.

the leaner . . .

food (two tablespoons)	cals	fat (g)	fat (%)	sat (g)	sodium (mg)
"lite" tartar sauce	60-100	1-4	9-60	1-2	70-420
hot dog sauce	30-60	1-3	30-45	0-1	180-220

"Lite" tartar sauces, which contain substantially less fat than regular tartar sauces, are available from Hellmann's and Golden Dipt.

the leanest . . .

food (two tablespoons)	cals	fat (g)	fat (%)	sat (g)	sodium (mg)
fast-food dipping sauce for nuggets	30-100	0-1	0-26	0	10-450
barbecue sauce	30-60	0-1	0-23	0	95-560
enchilada or taco sauce	5-20	0-1	0-36	0	115-300
picante sauce or salsa	5-15	0-1	0-75	0	5-750

food (two tablespoons)	cals	fat (g)	fat (%)	sat (g)	sodium (mg)
sweet and sour sauce	35-60	0	0	0	90-190
catsup	30-50	0	0	0	0-455
"lite" catsup	10-20	0	0	0	40-230
cocktail or seafood sauce	30-45	0	0	0	310-480
steak sauce	25-35	0	0	0	240-560
teriyaki sauce	30	0	0	0	1400
chili sauce	30	0	0	0	230-450
soy sauce (1 tablespoon)	5-15	0	0	0	330-960

All of these sauces contain little or no fat, and there are very few differences from brand to brand.

fat-skimming tips:

- avoid regular tartar sauce and béarnaise sauce

- use the following creatively: barbecue sauce, salsa, sweet and sour sauce, seafood and steak sauce, chili sauce, and soy sauce; they are fat-free and relatively low in calories

cals=calories; fat=grams of fat; %fat=percent of calories from fat; sat=grams of saturated fat; sodium=milligrams of sodium

Mustard and Other Hot or Spicy Sauces

These hot or spicy condiments are all low- or non-fat products, so it's only the calories that vary among your choices.

this affects the fat content:

addition of vegetable oils: higher-fat mustard and horseradish products have vegetable oil mixed in

things that do not affect the fat content:
flavor of mustard: honey, hot, spicy, brown, or other flavors of mustard all have the same fat content

degree of spiciness or hotness: The substances responsible for hot or spicy tastes are fat-free.

the fattiest . . .

food (one teaspoon)	cals	fat (g)	fat (%)	sat (g)	sodium (mg)
higher-fat horseradish sauces	15-30	2-3	72-90	0-1	35-55
higher-fat mustards	15-25	1-2	30-77	0	0-90
mustard-mayonnaise blend	10	1	75	0	70

Brands of higher-fat horseradish sauces, such as Kraft's Sauceworks, and brands of higher-fat mustards are blended with vegetable oil, while lower-fat horseradish and mustard contain little, if any, oil. Hellmann's Dijonnaise is a blend of mustard and mayonnaise, with more mustard than mayo.

the remainder . . .

food (one teaspoon)	cals	fat (g)	fat (%)	sat (g)	sodium (mg)
most mustards	5-15	0	0	0	0-165
most horseradish sauces	5	0	0	0	5-55
red hot sauce	0-5	0	0	0	135-260
soy sauce	0-5	0	0	0	210-350
Worcestershire sauce	0-5	0	0	0	55-60

Most mustards and horseradish sauces are fat-free. Brands

include French's, Grey Poupon, and Gulden's mustards, and Heluva Good and Gold's horseradish. Tabasco and Crystal are brands of red hot sauce, Lea & Perrins and French's brands of Worcestershire sauces.

fat-skimming tips:

- pass up higher-fat mustards and horseradish to avoid unnecessary fat

- use these hot or spicy sauces to liven up lower-fat dishes

see this page for:

224 catsup and soy sauce

cals=calories; fat=grams of fat; %fat=percent of calories from fat; sat=grams of saturated fat; sodium=milligrams of sodium

Gravy

Gravy has the image of being a very fatty, but civilized, way of sopping up greasy drippings from cooked meat. But the truth is that the gravies for sale in supermarkets and served in restaurants are surprisingly lean. There are even fat-free gravies available.

the fattiest . . .

food (quarter-cup serving)	cals	fat (g)	fat (%)	sat (g)	chol (mg)	sodium (mg)
chicken gravy	20-45	1-4	23-80	0-1	0	170-350
pork gravy	40	3	68	1	0	330
for comparison:						
butter or margarine	100	11	100	1-6	0-30	0-170

In comparison with butter or margarine, gravy is a far leaner topping for mashed potatoes or other foods. Brands of **chicken gravy** and **pork gravy** include Franco-American, KFC, Heinz, and Pepperidge Farm.

the leaner . . .

food (quarter-cup serving)	cals	fat (g)	fat (%)	sat (g)	chol (mg)	sodium (mg)
beef gravy	20-35	1-2	23-51	0-1	0	260-360
turkey gravy	25-40	1-2	30-60	0	0	260-370
mushroom gravy	20-30	1	23-45	0	0	290-370
onion gravy	25-35	1	13-36	0	0	280-350
brown gravy	10-25	1	23-75	0	0	100-330

These gravies are quite similar. Brands include Franco-American, Heinz, Pepperidge Farm, Pillsbury, and Knorr.

the leanest . . .

food (quarter-cup serving)	cals	fat (g)	fat (%)	sat (g)	chol (mg)	sodium (mg)
fat-free gravies	10-15	0	0	0	0	270-410
au jus	5-10	0	0	0	0	330-500

Fat-free gravies are available from Weight Watchers and Heinz. **Au jus,** such as Franco-American brand, is just the fat-free juice.

fat-skimming tip:
  • use gravy instead of butter on potatoes

see this page for:
  126 mashed potatoes

cals=calories; fat=grams of fat; %fat=percent of calories from fat; sat=grams of
saturated fat; sodium=milligrams of sodium

condiments

Pickles, Olives, Peppers, and Chilies
These are plant foods and, with the exception of olives, are naturally fat-free. Only their sodium contents are sometimes high.

things that affect the fat or calorie content:
packing in oil: Greek olives and some peppers are preserved in
oil and have an increased fat content as a result

   packing in sugar: sweet pickled cucumbers and vegetables
contain about 30 more calories per serving than kosher dill
pickles or unsweetened pickled vegetables

things that do not affect the fat or calorie content:
type of pickled vegetables, chilies, or peppers: all these foods
are low-calorie and fat-free

   refrigeration: pickles sold in refrigerated sections of supermarkets have the same calorie and fat content as those sold on
unrefrigerated shelves

   hot versus mild peppers: this doesn't affect the fat content

the fattiest . . .

food (30 grams)	cals	fat (g)	fat (%)	sat (g)	sodium (mg)
Greek olives	60-80	5-8	75-96	0-1	520-740
black or green olives	30-35	3-4	77-100	0	220-720
peppers packed in oil	30	2	60	0	30

Greek olives available in this country are often packed in oil, which raises their fat content. **Green olives** are fermented for months in brine. **Black olives** are cured for weeks. Two large green or black olives contain about 1 gram of fat. **Peppers packed in oil** pick up 2 grams of fat per serving.

the remainder . . .

food (30 grams)	cals	fat (g)	fat (%)	sat (g)	sodium (mg)
sweet pickles	35-45	0	0	0	20-260
sweet pickled vegetables	35	0	0	0	125-225
bread and butter pickles	20-30	0	0	0	110-220
capers	20	0	0	0	600
chilies	5-15	0	0	0	70-240
peppers	5-10	0	0	0	0-675
pimientos	5-10	0	0	0	5-40
kosher dill pickles	5	0	0	0	20-390
pickled vegetables	0-5	0	0	0	125-480

These are all low-calorie, fat-free, but often high-sodium foods.

cals=calories; fat=grams of fat; %fat=percent of calories from fat; sat=grams of saturated fat; sodium=milligrams of sodium

Relishes

Relishes are mixtures of fat-free ingredients: chopped vegetables, spices, and often vinegar. So it's not surprising that the end result is usually a fat-free condiment to complement or perk up a dish.

the choices . . .

food (one tablespoon)	cals	fat (g)	fat (%)	sat (g)	sodium (mg)
hot dog relish	30-40	0-1	0-30	0	255-260
chutney	35-100	0	0	0	420-440
cranberry sauce	40-50	0	0	0	5-10
pickle-based relish	5-40	0	0	0	100-415

These are all similar in their calorie and fat contents. Some **hot dog relishes** contain a small amount of vegetable oil. **Chutney** is a seasoned mixture of chopped fruits and vegetables. **Sauces of cranberries and other fruit** are available from Ocean Spray.

cals=calories; fat=grams of fat; %fat=percent of calories from fat; sat=grams of saturated fat; sodium=milligrams of sodium

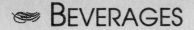 # BEVERAGES

fruit and vegetable juices, nectars, and cocktails
milk
flavored milks: chocolate milk, hot cocoa, and milkshakes
coffee, tea, and coffee beverages
coffee creamers
soft drinks: carbonated and non-carbonated
beer and wine
liquor and cocktails

Fruit and Vegetable Juices, Nectars, and Cocktails
Fruit and vegetable juices are enjoying a surge in popularity, with the interest in mechanical juicers and the scramble by food manufacturers to add real juice to food products. Fruit and vegetable juices are naturally low in fat, so only the calories vary among your choices.

things that affect the calorie content:
juice versus nectars and cocktails: since nectars and cocktails consist of sweetened fruit juice extracts, their calories usually exceed the calories in unsweetened 100 percent fruit juice

sweetening with sugar: some grapefruit and grape juices are sweetened with sugar—for grapefruit juice, this adds 15 to 20 calories per cup

vegetable versus fruit juices: since vegetables do not store sugar the way fruits do, juice extracted from vegetables con-

tains significantly less sugar and fewer calories than juices from
fruits

this doesn't affect the calorie content:
type of fruit: most fruits used for making juice contain similar
amounts of calories, about 100 to 135 calories per cup, with
the exceptions of prune and grape juice

those with the most calories . . .

food (one-cup serving)	cals	fat (g)	fat (%)	sat (g)	sodium (mg)
prune juice	160-185	0	0	0	5-15
cranberry juice cocktail	120-175	0	0	0	5-10
grape juice	130-165	0	0	0	5-20
fruit nectar	130-160	0	0	0	0-40
cranberry juice cocktail	135-145	0	0	0	5-10

Prune juice, a water extract of dried prunes, has the most
calories of any juice, in part because it contains more fruit and
less water than other juices. **Fruit nectars,** such as apricot or
peach, and **juice cocktails,** such as cranberry or grapefruit,
have sweeteners added to them, raising their calorie content.
Grape juice tends to have more calories than other juices,
especially if it is sweetened with additional sugar.

those with fewer calories . . .

food (one-cup serving)	cals	fat (g)	fat (%)	sat (g)	sodium (mg)
pineapple juice	130-135	0	0	0	5-10
breakfast beverages	95-120	0	0	0	10-25
orange juice	105-120	0	0	0	1-10

food (one-cup serving)	cals	fat (g)	fat (%)	sat (g)	sodium (mg)
grapefruit juice, sweetened	115	0	0	0	5
apple juice	100-115	0	0	0	5-10
grapefruit juice, unsweetened	95-100	0	0	0	2-5
carrot juice, canned	100	0	0	0	70

Brands of **breakfast beverages,** which are marketed as milder or more convenient alternatives to orange juice, include Tang and Awake.

those with the least calories . . .

food (one-cup serving)	cals	fat (g)	fat (%)	sat (g)	sodium (mg)
vegetable juice mixes or cocktails	45-60	0	0	0	320-885
tomato juice	40-55	0	0	0	690-880
"lite" cranberry juice cocktail	40-55	0	0	0	5-10

Vegetable juice cocktails, such as V-8 brand, consist of 100 percent juice, unlike fruit juice cocktails, which have sweeteners added. Note, however, the substantial amounts of sodium the vegetable cocktails contain.

TIP: The mere presence of fruit juice does not make a food wholesome and nutritious. Much of the fruit juice added to food products today consists of inexpensive apple, grape, and pear juices that have been stripped of their nutrients and flavor to make them easier to use in manufacturing. If you want all of the nutrients and wholesomeness of fruit juice, stick to products that don't rely on these processed fruit juices.

calorie-skimming tips:

- try vegetable juices—they have fewer calories than fruit juices

- pure fruit juices usually have fewer calories than fruit juice cocktails or nectars, so think *juice*.

cals=calories; fat=grams of fat; %fat=percent of calories from fat; sat=grams of saturated fat; sodium=milligrams of sodium

Milk

Milk has a big advantage over other foods derived from animals; its fat can be easily removed or skimmed. Since dairy fat is highly saturated, that's a big plus.

this affects the fat content:

fat content of milk: obviously, what percentage of the weight of the milk is milkfat—whole (about 3.3 percent milkfat by weight), 2 percent, 1 percent, or skim (about 0.5 percent milkfat)—affects the fat content per serving

things that do not affect the fat content:

fortification with protein, calcium, or Lactobacillus acidophilus: these add nutrients or potentially helpful bacteria, but do not increase the amount of fat

lactose reduction: treating milk with enzymes to lower its lactose content, making it more digestible for those who are lactose-intolerant, does not affect the fat content

dried versus liquid: dried skim milk has the same amount of fat as fluid skim milk

the fattiest . . .

food (one-cup serving)	cals	fat (g)	fat (%)	sat (g)	chol (mg)	sodium (mg)
whole milk, goat's	160-170	9	54	7	30-40	120-135
whole milk, cow's	150	8	49	5	35	120
soy milk, higher-fat	120-170	6-7	37-45	1	0	115-135

A cup of **goat's milk** contains one more gram of total fat and two more grams of saturated fat than **cow's milk. Soy milk** is made by soaking, grinding, and straining soybeans, which are naturally high in fat. Unless this fat is skimmed, soy milk will also be high in fat. Health Valley and Westsoy are two brands of higher-fat soy milk.

the less fatty . . .

food (one-cup serving)	cals	fat (g)	fat (%)	sat (g)	chol (mg)	sodium (mg)
2% milk	120-140	5	32-36	3	15-20	120-150
kefir	120	5	37	3	30	120
imitation milk	110	5	41	1	0	120
yogurt drinks	190-210	4	17-19	3	10	110
soy milk, medium-fat	130-140	3-4	18-26	1	0	115-130

Many low-fat and skim milks have dry milk ("non-fat dry milk solids") added to them to provide extra body or extra protein. This lifts the calorie content slightly, but not the fat. Most Americans do not need additional protein. **Kefir** is fermented milk. **Imitation milks** are typically manufactured from non-fat dried milk and vegetable oil. This use of vegetable oil instead of dairy fat results in a beverage with less saturated fat. However, because imitation milk may lack important nutrients, the American Academy of Pediatrics recommends that parents not feed it to infants or small children. Edensoy is a brand of **medium-fat soy milk;** Glen Oaks is a brand of **yogurt drink.**

the leanest . . .

food (one-cup serving)	cals	fat (g)	fat (%)	sat (g)	chol (mg)	sodium (mg)
1% milk	100-120	2-3	17-23	1-2	10	120-145
buttermilk, from 1% milk	100-120	2	17-23	1-2	10	120-145
soy milk, low-fat or fat-free	110-160	0-2	0-18	0-1	0	80-210
skim milk	85-100	0-1	5-6	0	5	125-145

True **buttermilk,** the fluid remaining after churning cream to make butter, is used primarily by the baking industry. The buttermilk found in stores is fermented from skim or low-fat milk. Westsoy Lite is a brand of **low-fat soy milk.**

TIP: The fat in cow's milk is about 62 percent saturated, which is high—beef and pork fat are about 40 percent saturated, chicken and turkey fat about 30 percent saturated. This means that the fat in other dairy foods, such as yogurt, cheese, butter, or ice cream, as well as the dairy fat added to foods, is 62 percent saturated.

fat-skimming tips:
- choose the lowest-fat milk you can—few people over two years of age need the large amounts of fat found in dairy foods

- if you do not care for the choices of 2 percent, 1 percent, or skim milk, try mixing two of these together to produce a different percent more to your liking. For instance, blending equal parts whole and 2 percent will make 2.7 percent milk, which is certainly better for you than drinking whole milk

see these pages for:
241 flavored milks and milkshakes
79 yogurt and cottage cheese

cals=calories; fat=grams of fat; %fat=percent of calories from fat; sat=grams of saturated fat; sodium=milligrams of sodium

Flavored Milks: Chocolate Milk, Hot Cocoa, and Milkshakes

Milk mixed with chocolate or other flavors—hot cocoa, chocolate milkshakes, and eggnog—are some of America's favorite, comforting beverages. Today, many are even low-fat or fat-free.

things that affect the fat content:
fat content of the milk: whether the milk is whole, low-fat, or skim determines *more than anything else* the amount of fat in the milk-flavored beverage

flavoring: milk mixes, syrups, and enhancers used to flavor milk add from 0 to 3 grams of fat per cup

this doesn't affect the fat content:
hot versus cold: the temperature of the beverage doesn't affect the fat content

the fattiest . . .

food (one-cup serving)	cals	fat (g)	fat (%)	sat (g)	chol (mg)	sodium (mg)
flavored whole milk	190-260	8-11	27-52	5-6	35-40	145-260
eggnog (4 oz. or half cup)	160-200	9	41-51	6	75	70-100
milkshakes						
higher-fat shakes	380-410	10	21-24		25	140
typical chocolate shake	200-310	5-8	16-36	1-5	20-30	140-235
typical vanilla shake	230-280	4-9	17-31	3-5	20-35	165-215
typical strawberry shake	180-295	5-8	16-35	3-4	15-25	165-200

Flavored whole milks are the result of combining whole milk with milk mixes and milk enhancers such as Nestle's Quik, Ovaltine, Carnation malted milk, and Hershey's cocoa and chocolate syrup. Ovaltine and Hershey's chocolate milk mix and chocolate syrup are fat-free. Nestle's Quik contains 1 gram of fat per serving, Carnation malted milk powder 2 grams, and Hershey's cocoa 3 grams. **Eggnog,** made from milk, eggs, and sweetener, is at least 6 percent milkfat. "Lite" formulations are now available (see less fatty options). **Milkshakes** traditionally are prepared from milk, syrup, and sometimes ice cream. Today, fast-food shakes are formulated principally from milk and sugar, with vegetable gums added to thicken the mixture. **Higher-fat milkshakes** are available at Dairy Queen restaurants. **Typical milkshakes** (which are equivalent to 2 percent or whole milk) are available at Wendy's, Burger King, and similar restaurants.

the less fatty . . .

food (one-cup serving)	cals	fat (g)	fat (%)	sat (g)	chol (mg)	sodium (mg)
flavored 2% milk	160-230	5-8	20-45	3-4	15-20	145-260
flavored 1% milk	140-220	2-5	8-32	1-2	20-25	145-260
hot cocoa mixes, regular	110-160	1-4	5-30	0-2	0-5	5-275
"lite" eggnog	110-130	2-3	14-25	1-2	20	60
chocolate-flavored drink	150	2	12	1	0	85

The same milk mixes and enhancers used above to flavor whole milk are used here with 1 percent and 2 percent milk. Swiss Miss is a national brand of **hot cocoa mixes** to prepare with hot water. **Chocolate-flavored drink,** such as the Hershey's brand sold in aseptic boxes, is manufactured from milk powder, hydrogenated vegetable oil, and sugar.

the leanest . . .

food (one-cup serving)	cals	fat (g)	fat (%)	sat (g)	chol (mg)	sodium (mg)
lower-fat fast-food shakes	225-245	1	4-5	1	10	130-185
lower-fat shake mixes	70-235	0-1	6-13	0	5	150-210
flavored skim milk	125-195	0-3	0-22	0-1	5-10	150-265
fat-free chocolate-flavor soft drink	130	0	0	0	0	160
"lite" cocoa mixes	35-95	0-1	0-23	0-1	0-5	120-150

Lower-fat fast-food milkshakes, available at McDonald's, are made from skim milk with virtually no added fat. Examples of **lower-fat shake mixes** are Weight Watchers and Alba brands. The skim milk is flavored with the same milk mixes and milk enhancers used with whole, 2 percent, and 1 percent milks above. Yoo-Hoo is a skim milk–based **fat-free chocolate-flavor soft drink. "Lite" cocoa mixes,** such as Swiss Miss and Carnation brands, contain less added fat and may use aspartame instead of sugar for sweetening.

fat-skimming tips:
- remember: it's usually the milk itself that contributes the most fat to flavored milks

- look for the milk mixes, such as Nestle's Quik, Ovaltine, and Hershey's chocolate syrup, that contain little or no fat

see these pages for:
238 different types of milks
39 instant breakfasts

cals=calories; fat=grams of fat; %fat=percent of calories from fat; sat=grams of saturated fat; sodium=milligrams of sodium

Coffee, Tea, and Coffee Beverages
Plain coffee and tea are naturally low in fat and calories. It's the creams, creamers, sweeteners, and other flavorings that add fat and calories to these beverages.

this affects the fat content:
kind of creamer used: milks, creams, and creamers can contain from 0 to 3 grams of fat per serving (see the section on creamers)

things that do not affect the fat content:
processing into instant or decaffeination: instant or decaffeinated beverages do not differ in their fat content from regular or caffeinated beverages

hot versus cold: this doesn't affect the fat content

chicory in coffee: this adds a few calories, but no fat

the fattiest . . .

food (one-cup serving)	cals	fat (g)	fat (%)	sat (g)	chol (mg)	sodium (mg)
gourmet coffee beverages	65-85	3-5	30-54	2-4	0	15-345
"lite" gourmet coffee beverages	40-45	3	51-60	2	0	140-370

Gourmet coffee beverages, such as General Foods International Coffees, have partially hydrogenated vegetable oil added to them to provide the sensation of richness. "Lite" versions have less of this fat added.

the less fatty . . .

food (one-cup serving)	cals	fat (g)	fat (%)	sat (g)	chol (mg)	sodium (mg)
bottled or canned specialty coffee	120-130	2-3	14-34	0-1	0-5	30-35
hot coffee or tea with cream (1T)	25-35	2-3	51-90	1-2	5-10	10-15
with cream (1T) and sugar (2t)	55-65	2-3	28-49	1-2	5-10	10-15
with creamer	15-25	1-2	36-90	0-1	0	10-15
with creamer and sugar (2t)	45-55	1-2	16-40	0-1	0	10-15
with milk (any kind) (1T)	10-15	0-1	0-90	0	1-2	15-20
with any milk (1T) and sugar (2t)	40-55	0-1	0-23	0	1-2	15-20

Bottled or canned specialty coffees have their cream and sweeteners already added. Brands include Chock o'ccino and Maxwell House's Iced Cappuccino. Milk, cream, or creamer can add from 0 to 3 grams of fat, and each teaspoon of sugar adds 16 calories.

the leanest . . .

food (one-cup serving)	cals	fat (g)	fat (%)	sat (g)	sodium (mg)
tea, instant, sweetened mix	85	0	0	0	0
tea, iced, sweetened mix	70-80	0	0	0	0-10
tea, iced, with 2t sugar	35	0	0	0	5-10
coffee substitute (grain)	10-15	0	0	0	0-10
coffee with chicory	10	0	0	0	15
tea, iced, plain mix	5	0	0	0	5-10
black coffee or brewed tea	1-5	0	0	0	5-10

The only significant source of calories in these beverages is sugar. **Coffee substitutes,** such as Postum, are fat-free as well as caffeine-free because they are made from grains such as barley and wheat. **Chicory,** a roasted, ground root that looks like coffee but is cheaper, has no fat and few calories.

TIP: Coffee and tea can interfere with the absorption of iron from food or supplements. If you need the iron, either don't drink these beverages within an hour of eating an iron-rich meal or taking an iron-containing supplement, or make sure the meal or supplement contains at least 50 milligrams of vitamin C.

fat-skimming tip:
 • the fat content of most coffee and tea is determined by

the cream or creamer added, so limit the cream or learn
to enjoy beverages without it

see these pages for:
247 creamers
217 sugar and other sweeteners

cals=calories; fat=grams of fat; %fat=percent of calories from fat; sat=grams of
saturated fat; sodium=milligrams of sodium

Coffee Creamers
The creams, milks, and non-dairy concoctions used to lighten
coffee and tea are in most coffee and tea beverages the only
source of fat.

things that affect the fat content:
kind of milk, cream, or creamer: whether the milk is whole,
low-fat, or skim; the cream full-fat or half-and-half; or the
creamer full-fat or reduced-fat is critical

adding flavor to creamer: creamers with specialty flavors,
such as Irish creme or almond mocha, are usually higher-fat

things that do not affect the fat content:
powder versus liquid creamer: either can be higher-fat or
lower-fat

the fattiest . . .

food (one tablespoon)	cals	fat (g)	fat (%)	sat (g)	chol (mg)	sodium (mg)
coffee or table cream	30	3	89	2	10	5
flavored creamers	40-60	2-3	45	2-3	0	5-15
half-and-half	20	2	80	1	5	5

Coffee cream, also known as **light cream** or **table cream,** is cream with a fat content of 18 percent to 30 percent by weight (that's about 5 to 9 times the concentration of fat in whole milk). **Half-and-half,** a mixture of milk and cream, contains 10.5 percent to 18 percent milkfat by weight. **Coffee creamers** are formulated from milk ingredients and vegetable fat. Coffee Mate has a line of **flavored creamers.**

the less fatty . . .

food (one serving)	cals	fat (g)	fat (%)	sat (g)	chol (mg)	sodium (mg)
most regular coffee creamers	10-20	1-2	45-90	0-1	0	5-10
evaporated milk, whole (1T)	20	1	51	1	5	15
whole milk (1T)	10	1	49	0	2	10

Note that **most regular coffee creamers,** such as Cremora and Coffee Mate brands, contain more fat than a comparable amount of **whole milk. Evaporated milk,** both whole and skim, can be used to lighten coffee.

the leanest . . .

food (one serving)	cals	fat (g)	fat (%)	sat (g)	chol (mg)	sodium (mg)
"lite" powder or liquid creamers	10	0-1	0-56	0	0	5-15
evaporated skim milk (1T)	10	0	2	0	1	15
2% milk (1T)	10	0.3	35	0	1	10
1% milk (1T)	5	0.2	23	0	1	10
skim milk (1T)	5	0.1	5	0	0	10

"Lite" creamers include Coffee Mate Lite and Cremora Lite. The small amount of fat in **2 percent, 1 percent, and skim milk** does not reach 1 gram in a tablespoon.

fat-skimming tip:
  • use milk—even whole milk has less total fat and less saturated fat than most regular creamers

see this page for:
  244 coffee and tea

cals=calories; fat=grams of fat; %fat=percent of calories from fat; sat=grams of saturated fat; sodium=milligrams of sodium

Soft Drinks: Carbonated and Non-Carbonated

Soft drinks now have surpassed milk as the most popular beverage in the United States. The average American drinks at least 16 ounces each day.

Soft drinks in this section include all the carbonated and non-carbonated beverages that are not fruit juices, alcohol, or drinks made from milk ingredients. Since these soft drinks are all fat-free, the calories are what vary among your choices.

this affects the calorie content:
whether drink is sweetened with sugar or with a sugar substitute: eight ounces of a typical soft drink sweetened with sugar or corn syrup contains about 105 calories, or the equivalent of 6.5 teaspoons of sugar; a 12-ounce can or bottle contains the equivalent of 10 teaspoons of sugar. Sweetening with a sugar substitute such as aspartame, on the other hand, adds fewer than five calories

things that do not affect the calorie content:
carbonation versus non–carbonation: this doesn't raise or lower the calories

choice of flavors: there are only small differences in the calorie contents for different flavors

addition of fruit juice: some soft drinks are manufactured with small amounts of fruit juice, but in most cases the amounts are too small to matter much

sucrose versus corn syrup: both have similar amounts of calories

container: drinks in cans, bottles, and boxes, and from mixes, have similar amounts of calories

those with the most calories . . .

food (8-oz. or one-cup serving)	cals	fat (g)	fat (%)	sat (g)	sodium (mg)
carbonated					
cream soda	125	0	0	0	30
orange or grapefruit flavored	105-120	0	0	0	10-35
grape	105-125	0	0	0	10-40
root beer	100-115	0	0	0	1-35
colas	95-105	0	0	0	1-10
lemon flavored	95-105	0	0	0	5-40
Seven-Up brand	95-100	0	0	0	20
"pepper" flavored	100	0	0	0	25
ginger ale	80-95	0	0	0	5-25

food (8-oz. or one-cup serving)	cals	fat (g)	fat (%)	sat (g)	sodium (mg)
non-carbonated fruit-flavored drinks in bottle, box, can, or from mix	80-140	0	0	0	5-55

All of these drinks contain from 80 to 125 calories per cup, whether they are carbonated, flavored with fruit juice, bottled, canned, or boxed, or whether they are colas, ginger ales, or other flavors.

those with fewer calories . . .

food (8-oz. or one-cup serving)	cals	fat (g)	fat (%)	sat (g)	sodium (mg)
sports drinks	50-60	0	0	0	55-110
low-calorie fruit juice–based drinks	25-55	0	0	0	5-45
"lite" drinks, carbonated sodas, juices	0-15	0	0	0	15-45

Sports drinks, such as Gatorade, contain less sugar and more sodium and potassium than regular soft drinks. **Low-calorie fruit juice–based drinks,** such as the Tropicana Twister brands, are blends of fruit juice, water, flavorings, and a sugar substitute. **"Lite" drinks, carbonated sodas, and juices** are the "diet" and very low-calorie beverages sweetened with a sugar substitute, usually aspartame. Among the hundreds of brands are Diet Coke (soda) and Crystal Light (drink mix).

see this page for:
235 fruit juice

cals=calories; fat=grams of fat; %fat=percent of calories from fat; sat=grams of saturated fat; sodium=milligrams of sodium

Beer and Wine

Beer and wine do not contain any fat, so only the alcohol and calorie contents vary among the choices. Alcohol itself is a relatively high-calorie substance. Pure alcohol contains about 7 calories per gram, midway between the 9 calories per gram that pure fat has, and the 4 calories per gram that pure carbohydrates and protein have.

this affects the calorie content:
alcohol content: the more alcohol in a beverage, the more calories, so the choices with the least calories are the lower-alcohol and non-alcohol beers and wines

this doesn't affect the calorie content:
type of grain or grapes: whether a beer is brewed from barley or rice, or a wine fermented from red or white grapes, does not affect the calorie content

those with the most calories . . .

food (12 oz.)	cals	fat (g)	fat (%)	sat (g)	sodium (mg)
malt liquor	150-170	0	0	0	
ale	155-165	0	0	0	
regular beer	135-165	0	0	0	20-25

Both **malt liquor** and **ale** have a higher alcohol content than **regular beer,** hence their higher number of calories.

those with fewer calories . . .

food (one serving)	cals	fat (g)	fat (%)	sat (g)	sodium (mg)
"lite" beer (12 oz.)	70-135	0	0	0	10
table wine, red or white (4 oz.)	80-115	0	0	0	5
champagne (4 oz.)	105	0	0	0	

"Lite" beers have either been brewed to a lower alcohol content, or they have had some of their alcohol removed after brewing. On average, a brand's "lite" formulation contains about 45 fewer calories per 12 ounces than its regular beer.

those with the least calories . . .

food (one serving)	cals	fat (g)	fat (%)	sat (g)	sodium (mg)
dessert wine (2 oz.)	55-95	0	0	0	5
sweet wine (2 oz.)	85	0	0	0	
vermouth (2 oz.)	70-85	0	0	0	
non-alcoholic beer (12 oz.)	50-75	0	0	0	0
wine cooler (4 oz.)	50-65	0	0	0	
"lite" wine (4 oz.)	55	0	0	0	
wine spritzer (4 oz.)	50	0	0	0	
alcohol-free wine or champagne (4 oz.)	30-40	0	0	0	5-15

Ounce for ounce, **dessert wines** have more calories than table wines because they are fortified with additional alcohol in the form of brandy. **Sweet wines** are fortified with additional alcohol and contain extra unfermented sugar. **Wine**

coolers and **wine spritzers** are diluted with fruit juice or carbonated water. **Non-alcoholic beer,** such as Pabst NA and Kingsbury brands, and **alcohol-free wine and champagne,** such as St. Regis and Sutter Home brands, have only one-third to one-half the calories of regular beer or wine.

calorie-skimming tips:
check alcohol content: the lower the alcohol content, the fewer the calories

see this page for:
   254 liquor and cocktails

cals=calories; fat=grams of fat; %fat=percent of calories from fat; sat=grams of saturated fat; sodium=milligrams of sodium

Liquor and Cocktails
Only one popular cocktail contains fat, the piña colada. All of the others, as well as all distilled liquors, are fat-free, so it's the calories that vary among the choices.

things that affect the calorie content:
alcohol content: the more alcohol, or the greater the proof, the more calories

   choice of mixer: fruit juices and tonic water have more calories than club soda or seltzer

this doesn't affect the fat content:
choice of distilled liquor: gin, vodka, rum, whiskey, scotch, and other liquors have the same amount of calories

one with fat . . .

food (4.5 oz)	cals	fat (g)	fat (%)	sat (g)	sodium (mg)
piña colada	240-260	2-3	9-10	1	10

The fat in **piña coladas** is contributed by coconut cream.

one with more calories . . .

food (7 oz.)	cals	fat (g)	fat (%)	sat (g)	sodium (mg)
screwdriver	160	0	0	0	0

The large amount of orange juice in a **screwdriver** boosts the calories.

some with fewer calories . . .

food (one serving)	cals	fat (g)	fat (%)	sat (g)	sodium (mg)
medium-calorie cocktails gin and tonic (7.5 oz.)	130-135	0	0	0	5-10
tequila sunrise (5.5 oz.)					
90 to 100 proof liquors (1.5 oz.) gin	110-125	0	0	0	0
vodka					
rum					
whiskey					
scotch					

those with the least calories . . .

food (one serving)	cals	fat (g)	fat (%)	sat (g)	sodium (mg)
80 to 86 proof liquors (1.5 oz.)	100-105	0	0	0	0
whiskey					
rum					
vodka					
lower-calorie cocktails	90-105	0	0	0	0-305
Bloody Mary (5 oz.)					
whiskey sour (3 oz.)					
daiquiri (2 oz.)					
Tom Collins (7.5 oz.)					
Manhattan (2 oz.)					
martini (2.5 oz.)					
bourbon and soda (4 oz.)					

see this page for:
252 beer and wine

cals=calories; fat=grams of fat; %fat=percent of calories from fat; sat=grams of
saturated fat; sodium=milligrams of sodium